HC 79. E5 ECO

QMW Library

23 1161253 4

KV-638-009

ECO-EFFICIENCY

DATE DUE FOR RETURN

NEW ACCESSIONS

CANCELLED

16 MAY 2001

WITH
FR
QMU

WITHDRAWN
FROM STOCK
QMUL LIBRARY

ORGANISAT   NT

ORGANISATION FOR ECONOMIC CO-OPERATION AND DEVELOPMENT

Pursuant to Article 1 of the Convention signed in Paris on 14th December 1960, and which came into force on 30th September 1961, the Organisation for Economic Co-operation and Development (OECD) shall promote policies designed:

- to achieve the highest sustainable economic growth and employment and a rising standard of living in Member countries, while maintaining financial stability, and thus to contribute to the development of the world economy;
- to contribute to sound economic expansion in Member as well as non-member countries in the process of economic development; and
- to contribute to the expansion of world trade on a multilateral, non-discriminatory basis in accordance with international obligations.

The original Member countries of the OECD are Austria, Belgium, Canada, Denmark, France, Germany, Greece, Iceland, Ireland, Italy, Luxembourg, the Netherlands, Norway, Portugal, Spain, Sweden, Switzerland, Turkey, the United Kingdom and the United States. The following countries became Members subsequently through accession at the dates indicated hereafter: Japan (28th April 1964), Finland (28th January 1969), Australia (7th June 1971), New Zealand (29th May 1973), Mexico (18th May 1994), the Czech Republic (21st December 1995), Hungary (7th May 1996), Poland (22nd November 1996) and Korea (12th December 1996). The Commission of the European Communities takes part in the work of the OECD (Article 13 of the OECD Convention).

Publié en français sous le titre :
ÉCO-EFFICIENCE

© OECD 1998
Permission to reproduce a portion of this work for non-commercial purposes or classroom use should be obtained through the Centre français d'exploitation du droit de copie (CFC), 20, rue des Grands-Augustins, 75006 Paris, France, Tel. (33-1) 44 07 47 70, Fax (33-1) 46 34 67 19, for every country except the United States. In the United States permission should be obtained through the Copyright Clearance Center, Customer Service, (508)750-8400, 222 Rosewood Drive, Danvers, MA 01923 USA, or CCC Online: http://www.copyright.com/. All other applications for permission to reproduce or translate all or part of this book should be made to OECD Publications, 2, rue André-Pascal, 75775 Paris Cedex 16. France.

FOREWORD

In 1995 the OECD held a workshop in Rosendal, Norway, to clarify several concepts related to sustainable consumption and production. Participants discussed "ecospace", "ecological footprints", "ecological rucksacks", "green accounting" and "eco-efficiency". Most of the concepts are used to provide indicators and benchmarks of progress towards sustainability and to make comparisons among products, firms and communities.

Workshop participants identified "eco-efficiency" as one of the most useful of these concepts. They found that it was a flexible and pragmatic approach, suitable for translating into action by governments, industry, other organisations and households. However, they felt that the term "eco-efficiency" was insufficient on its own as a basis for policy making. A wider understanding would be needed of the links between economic activity and environmental damage, driving forces of change, and the psychological and ethical motives of producer and consumer behaviour.

At their February 1996 meeting, OECD Environment Ministers reviewed environmental progress in Member countries. They concluded that, although pollution has been reduced over the last 25 years, further effort is needed to address global challenges such as climate change and biodiversity loss. Current environment policies are unlikely to be sufficient to cope with the environmental challenges of the next century. These challenges demand a paradigm shift in governments, businesses and households. The Ministerial Communiqué also stated that :

Eco-efficiency is a (...) strategy which Ministers viewed as highly promising to enable industry, governments and households to decouple pollutant release and resource use from economic activity. Ministers noted the existence of studies which suggested that efficiency improvements of a factor of ten were both necessary and achievable in the next thirty years. They encouraged the OECD to work with the World Business Council for Sustainable Development and others to assess the potential of eco-efficiency to this end.

As a response to the Ministerial Communiqué, this report:

- *examines past trends,* in order to evaluate the extent to which economic activity is coupled to pollutant releases and resource use;

- *reviews initiatives* to improve eco-efficiency at the firm, community and household level and identifies ways in which governments can provide encouragement and guidance;

- *evaluates the potential* for economy-wide improvements in eco-efficiency, and identifies government policies that can help achieve that potential;

- *suggests strategies* that governments can pursue in partnership through the OECD.

The report has been prepared with substantial input from delegates to the OECD Pollution Prevention and Control Group. It also draws on two workshops organised by the OECD. The first workshop, in Berlin in July 1997, explored the application of the concept of eco-efficiency in the transport sector. The second, in Paris in September 1997, undertook a broader review of existing efforts to apply eco-efficiency and considered the role of governments in fostering eco-efficiency.

The council of the OECD agreed to the derestriction of this report on 16 March, 1998.

CONTENTS

EXECUTIVE SUMMARY

In their 1996 meeting, OECD Environment Ministers observed that a strategy to improve "eco-efficiency" might enable industry, governments and households to decouple pollutant release and resource use from economic activity. They encouraged the OECD to assess the potential of eco-efficiency in the light of studies suggesting that factor-of-ten efficiency improvements are both necessary and possible in the next thirty years.

WHAT IS ECO-EFFICIENCY?

In the face of growing global environmental challenges, there is an urgent need for instruments that can translate sustainability requirements into working targets. Human pressures on the environment depend on both the volume of consumption and production, and the environmental pressure per unit produced and consumed. Eco-efficiency expresses *the efficiency with which ecological resources are used to meet human needs*. It can be considered as a ratio of an output divided by an input: the "output" being the value of products and services produced by a firm, a sector, or the economy as a whole, and the "input" being the sum of environmental pressures generated by the firm, sector or economy. Measuring eco-efficiency depends on identifying indicators of both input and output.

"Eco-efficiency" is the efficiency with which ecological resources are used to meet human needs

STRATEGIES TO IMPROVE ECO-EFFICIENCY

Improving eco-efficiency involves: developing indicators and goals; innovation to reach the goals; and monitoring the results

The World Business Council for Sustainable Development (WBCSD) has pioneered a business strategy to improve eco-efficiency that involves:

a) Developing indicators and goals.

b) Working towards the goals through a process of innovation in technology, modes of organisation and ways of thinking.

c) Monitoring the indicators and modifying the strategy if necessary.

Approaches based on indicators, targets, innovation and monitoring have considerable potential, but different meanings for different actors. Such strategies have been adopted by governments, community organisations and households. This report evaluates experience with such strategies to improve eco-efficiency in firms, local governments and communities. It also considers the role of national governments, both in encouraging local initiatives and in developing their own strategies to improve eco-efficiency economy-wide.

BUSINESS GOALS, INDICATORS AND TARGETS

WBCSD's goals for eco-efficiency require firms to enter into partnerships with governments, customers and suppliers

WBCSD explains eco-efficiency goals at the firm level as follows:

Eco-efficiency is reached by the delivery of competitively-priced goods and services that satisfy human needs and bring quality of life, while progressively reducing ecological impacts and resource intensity throughout the life cycle, to a level at least in line with the earth's estimated carrying capacity.

This statement includes broad social objectives and environmental constraints. Such goals require government involvement, and also depend on businesses entering into partnerships with their customers and suppliers.

Seven criteria for eco-efficiency, listed in the box, have been embodied in a variety of qualitative indicators developed by firms. Many firms have also developed targets for reducing their intensity of material use, energy consumption and toxic emissions per unit of production. They monitor progress towards these targets and release the results in their annual environmental reports. Few have developed quantitative indicators or targets for concepts such as "service intensity" (*i.e.* the quality of the service they provide to their customers), or for reducing impacts over the life-cycle.

Many firms have developed indicators and targets for improving eco-efficiency, but few address the whole life-cycle

---

WBCSD criteria for eco-efficiency:

a) minimise the material intensity of goods and services;

b) minimise the energy intensity of goods and services;

c) minimise toxic dispersion;

d) enhance material recyclability;

e) maximise the use of renewable resources;

f) extend product durability;

g) increase the service intensity of goods and services.

POTENTIAL FOR INITIATIVES BY FIRMS AND COMMUNITIES TO IMPROVE ECO-EFFICIENCY

The OECD has studied numerous initiatives to improve eco-efficiency at the firm or community level. Under current market conditions and environment policy, manufacturers have found profitable ways to reduce their use of materials, energy and water per unit of production by 10-40%. Initiatives in the services sector, local governments and households achieve similar savings. Firms have also demonstrated technologies that cut the use or emission of toxic substances by 90% or more, although these technologies are not always put into place.

10-40% reductions in material and energy inputs are often profitable

A few firms have taken initiatives to reduce environmental impacts during and after the use of products, for example by recovering used equipment and re-using durable components. Initiatives that address impacts over the full life-cycle offer the greatest potential for reducing pollution and resource use economy-wide.

ROLE OF GOVERNMENT IN ENCOURAGING INITIATIVES BY FIRMS AND COMMUNITIES

Government incentives and support can increase the potential for improving eco-efficiency at the level of the firm

A major task for governments is to enhance the consistency of efforts at the firm and household level, by establishing a policy framework that reduces the gap between private and social aims. Economic incentives to reduce pollution would improve the profitability of savings in energy and materials. Meanwhile, the technical potential for reducing toxic emissions is only likely to be achieved through government incentives and regulations. Initiatives to reduce environmental pressure throughout the product life-cycle most commonly occur where governments have introduced the concept of "extended producer responsibility".

New options to improve eco-efficiency will become available in the future as a result of innovation. Governments can create a good "climate for innovation" by: supporting co-operative research and experimentation by firms, local governments and others; stimulating new niche markets through public procurement and tendering policies; promoting networks among companies, local governments and other organisations; providing information to bridge communication gaps; and supporting the development of standard monitoring and reporting procedures.

ECONOMY-WIDE INDICATORS AND TARGETS

Eco-efficiency targets should be based on specific environmental goals appropriate to local circumstances

The "Factor 10 Club" argues that the intensity of material and energy use in the economy should be reduced by a factor of ten in industrialised countries over the next 30-50 years, in order halve global CO_2 emissions while allowing for continuing economic growth. Although "Factor 10" may serve as an effective slogan to mobilise political support, it should not be taken literally, as energy and material use are only loosely related to specific environmental problems other than CO_2 emissions.

National and local sustainable development goals and indicators are needed to address environmental challenges that vary among countries and locations. Eco-efficiency targets can supplement such goals, but they also need to be tailored to reflect sectoral trends and specific environmental challenges. OECD governments are increasingly working with stakeholders to develop quantita-

tive benchmarks and goals for sustainable development. Stakeholder involvement can help in choosing among complex and conflicting priorities, and also eases the subsequent introduction of
policies to achieve the targets.

RECENT TRENDS IN POLLUTION RELEASE
AND RESOURCE USE ECONOMY-WIDE

Many indicators of economic and quality-of-life "output" have
improved in the last ten years in OECD countries. As the figure
below shows, some indicators of eco-efficiency "input", such as
emissions of regulated pollutants, have improved too. However,
many indicators have worsened, including CO_2 emissions, waste
generation, and water consumption.

*Some pollution
trends are
improving, others
are worsening*

◆ **OECD trends in GDP and a range of eco-efficiency "input" indicators**
Average annual percentage change, 1985-1995

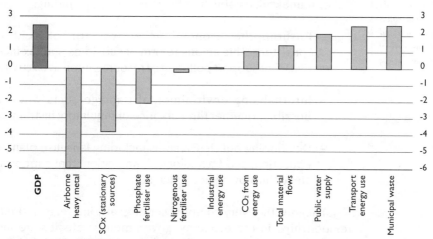

Note: Figures relate to all OECD Member countries except: airborne heavy metals and total material flows, which are for
Germany, Japan and United States only; public water supply is for Canada, France, Germany, Japan, United Kingdom and United
States only, 1985-1990.
Sources: OECD Statistics, World Resources Institute.

POTENTIAL FOR IMPROVING ECO-EFFICIENCY
THROUGHOUT THE ECONOMY

High input prices and strong competitive pressure can contribute to rapid productivity increases...

Industries have achieved very rapid improvements in some eco-efficiency indicators in the past, motivated by strong competitive pressures, high input prices, technical and resource constraints, or government regulation. During the high oil price years of 1974-1986, the energy intensity of air traffic fell by 4% per year, and OECD industry reduced its oilconsumption per unit of output by 8% per year. Over the longer term, OECD economies have achieved average labour productivity increases of 2-3% per year over 200 years, increasing incomes ten-fold while halving working hours.

... but not necessarily to less pollution

Eco-efficiency improvements alone do not necessarily reduce environmental pressure. In the case of air travel, traffic grew by nearly 8% per year between 1974 and 1988, so that energy use increased by nearly 4% per year.

ROLE OF GOVERNMENT IN PROMOTING
ECO-EFFICIENCY ECONOMY-WIDE

Consistent economy-wide change would require a broad framework of policy incentives

Economy-wide improvements in eco-efficiency depend on the policy framework established by government, including:

– Ensuring that economic incentives are coherent and consistent. This entails reform of subsidies and tax incentives that support polluting or resource-intensive activities.

– Internalising environmental damage costs wherever possible, whether through price or regulatory instruments.

– Developing policies in areas including land-use planning, education, and technological innovation, that support the aim of improving eco-efficiency.

Faced with a very complex set of goals, interests and interrelationships in the economy, government strategies are more likely to succeed if they are: broadly based and coherent, using a mix of instruments; inclusive of stakeholders in policy design and implementation; tolerant of experimentation and occasional failure; and adaptive, using monitoring and feedback mechanisms to adjust measures when necessary.

NEXT STEPS

Work in four areas could support the development of policies to improve eco-efficiency:

1. identification or development of transparent, comprehensive indicators of eco-efficiency as part of a broader set of sustainable development indicators;

2. analysis of current and future environmental pressures, in order to establish the changes in technological, structural and behavioural trends needed to decouple pollutant release and resource use from economic activity on a global basis;

3. an exchange of information among OECD Member countries on their experiences with policies supporting eco-efficiency improvements through innovation in technology, behaviour and institutions;

4. sectoral and economy-wide studies of the environmental and economic effects of policies and programmes to improve eco-efficiency.

1. INTRODUCTION: WHAT IS ECO-EFFICIENCY?

In the face of growing global environmental challenges, there is an urgent need for instruments that can translate sustainability requirements into working targets. Human pressures on the environment depend on both the volume of consumption and production, and the environmental pressure per unit produced and consumed. This report evaluates experience with strategies to improve "eco-efficiency", which is taken to mean the efficiency with which environmental resources are used to meet human needs. Eco-efficiency can be considered as a ratio of an output divided by an input: the "output" being the value of products and services produced by a firm, a sector, or the economy as a whole, and the "input" being the sum of environmental pressures generated by the firm, sector or economy.

Eco-efficiency is an idea that is beginning to take hold in parts of the business world in OECD countries. It has been described as "the business contribution to sustainable development".

The term "eco-efficiency" is used in different ways depending on the context. Its concrete definition and measurement depends on identifying indicators of both input and output. Such indicators are more easily defined for firms and for some types of government activity than they are for many types of household activity.

The Business Council for Sustainable Development (BCSD, later WBCSD*) adopted "eco-efficiency" as a business concept in 1992, in its report to the Rio Earth Summit (Schmidheiny, 1992). WBCSD describes eco-efficiency as a combination of ecological and economic efficiency.

Practitioners of the WBCSD approach adopt a strategy that includes several common components:

- They develop specific indicators and criteria or goals for improving their eco-efficiency.

---

* BCSD later merged with the World Industry Council for the Environment to form WBCSD.

- They work towards their goals through innovation in technology, practices and ways of thinking.

- They monitor the indicators and modify the strategy if necessary.

This strategy combines the features of many other approaches and themes in environment policy. These include "pollution prevention", "cleaner production", "life-cycle management", "environmental management systems" and others. It goes beyond these approaches in explicitly incorporating broader social priorities. This combination seems to make eco-efficiency a useful concept for businesses, and also for government officials working with businesses.

By bringing together environmental and economic goals, eco-efficiency is an essential element, but not the whole, of sustainable development. The Brundtland Commission and the Rio Declaration (UNCED, 1992) also emphasised the need to improve equity, reduce poverty, encourage democracy and support human rights. Whereas WBCSD aims to use eco-efficiency improvements to reduce resource use and environmental damage to levels within the earth's carrying capacity, the Brundtland Commission also emphasised the need to build up stocks of natural capital.

In recent years, the term "eco-efficiency" has come into more widespread use in governments and in environmental non-governmental organisations (NGOs). The OECD has also identified eco-efficiency as potentially one of the most useful of a range of new concepts linked to sustainable development (OECD, 1997a).

Eco-efficiency improvements can take several forms. For example:

- *Adoption* of existing better practices and technology can improve environmental performance and increase profits or reduce costs. Most examples of eco-efficiency improvements in the literature take this form. Such initiatives are often called "win-win" and offer a moderate potential for environmental benefits, although there is a risk of a "rebound effect", where lower costs stimulate more consumption and production, leading to greater environmental impacts. Governments use a variety of policies to encourage the uptake of "best practice" and to try to avoid the rebound effect.

- *Development* of new practices and technology can also improve both environmental and economic performance. There are several examples of such initiatives in the business literature on eco-efficiency. The essentially creative nature of these developments makes it harder to assess their potential or to design policies to stimulate them. Although the innovations are often characterised as "win-win" for the economy and the environment, it is not known how policies to stimulate innovation for *environmental* purposes affect innovation for *product development* or cost-cutting purposes. Again, the rebound effect can reduce any environmental benefits.

- *Responses to changes in market conditions* can improve eco-efficiency. Increased competition, resource constraints or price changes can make it profitable for firms to shift towards more eco-efficient technology and practices. Once the market conditions have changed, such improvements are "win-win" opportunities for some firms, but may be "win-lose" for others, sometimes to the extent that they go out of business. Governments considering stimulating eco-efficiency improvements through changes in their regulation of markets or their tax structure have to consider the economic costs associated with some environmental benefits.

In February 1996, the OECD Environment Ministers identified improving eco-efficiency as a promising route to enable industry, governments and households to decouple pollutant release and resource use from economic activity. Ministers also noted studies which suggested that factor-of-ten efficiency improvements were both necessary and achievable in the next thirty years. They encouraged the OECD to work with the World Business Council for Sustainable Development (WBCSD) and others to assess the potential of eco-efficiency to this end.

This report aims to respond to the ministers in several steps:

- Section 2 reviews a wide range of initiatives by firms, national and local governments and other organisations that aim to improve "eco-efficiency" or make use of the WBCSD approach. It also considers policies to encourage such initiatives.

- Section 3 looks at the role of government in improving eco-efficiency economy-wide. The section considers whether "Factor 10" is an appropriate target for eco-efficiency improvements, in the light of current trends in environmental pressures and resource use.

- Finally, Section 4 summarises the overall role of governments in relation to "eco-efficiency" and identifies next steps for the OECD and Member countries.

In responding to the OECD Environment Ministers' request, the main purpose of the report is *to consider strategies for improving eco-efficiency* and evaluate their actual and potential effectiveness when applied by firms, households, governments and others. The report also illustrates the many forms that innovation can take, and discusses the role of government in encouraging changes in technology, practices and ways of thinking.

17

2. IMPROVING ECO-EFFICIENCY IN FIRMS AND COMMUNITIES

The OECD has identified numerous business, local government and community initiatives to reduce pollution, resource use and costs while improving products and services. Only a few of these initiatives were originally designed to improve "eco-efficiency": many were designed for "waste minimisation", "pollution prevention" or other objectives. Improving eco-efficiency will include such efforts and many others. This section identifies and discusses some of these initiatives, examines their effectiveness in improving eco-efficiency in firms and communities, and considers their potential for broader application.

The initiatives discussed in this section aim to change the technology, institutions or behaviour involved in meeting human needs. Change can come about

◆ Figure 1. **The technical and social dimensions of innovation**

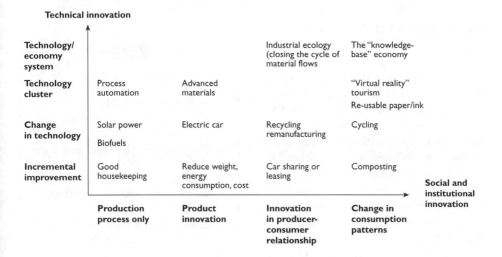

Technical innovation				
Technology/ economy system			Industrial ecology (closing the cycle of material flows	The "knowledge-base" economy
Technology cluster	Process automation	Advanced materials		"Virtual reality" tourism Re-usable paper/ink
Change in technology	Solar power Biofuels	Electric car	Recycling remanufacturing	Cycling
Incremental improvement	Good housekeeping	Reduce weight, energy consumption, cost	Car sharing or leasing	Composting
	Production process only	**Product innovation**	**Innovation in producer-consumer relationship**	**Change in consumption patterns**

Social and institutional innovation →

Note: The "technical innovation" scale is based on a taxonomy by Freeman and Perez (1988). Innovation is defined here to include the application (diffusion) of existing technology.

through the development of a completely new technology or practice, or through the adoption of an approach that has already been used elsewhere. The latter is often called "diffusion".

Innovations can be described and classified in many ways. Figure I organises some examples in two dimensions: the degree of *technical innovation* and the location in the product cycle of *social and institutional innovation*. The social aspects of technical change are often under-emphasised, although technical change and behavioural change cannot be separated. All changes in technology require behavioural change somewhere in the life-cycle of a good or service – during design, production, use, maintenance or disposal/recovery. Large technical changes generally involve some change in the product or service received by the consumer. The more extensive the behavioural change required, the harder it is to introduce a new technology. The discussion in this section proceeds from production process changes through to changes in consumption patterns.

The section starts with a discussion of the indicators and criteria used by firms in their strategies to improve eco-efficiency, and follows with a review of the changes they have introduced in their production processes, products and relationships with consumers. It continues by reviewing initiatives by other actors, including local governments and communities. Finally, it examines the role of national governments in supporting the process of change at the firm and community level, including support for monitoring systems.

2.1. BUSINESS INITIATIVES

WBCSD and its member companies have agreed a definition of eco-efficiency which is given in Box 1. They have also developed strategies for improving eco-efficiency, through numerous publications and workshops (e.g. BCSD, 1993; WBCSD, 1995). Although their focus has been mainly on eco-efficiency at the level of the individual firm, the definition also emphasises broader social objectives and environmental constraints. WBCSD has described eco-efficiency as creating "a needed bridge between the macro-level concept of 'sustainable develop-

---

Box I

WBCSD definition:

"Eco-efficiency is reached by

- *the delivery of competitively-priced goods and services;*

- *that satisfy human needs and bring quality of life;*

- *while progressively reducing ecological impacts and resource intensity throughout the life cycle;*

- *to a level at least in line with the earth's estimated carrying capacity."*

Source: BCSD, 1993.

ment' and the micro-level of corporate behaviour". Firms working alone cannot define or address "human needs" and "quality of life". Nor can they reduce ecological impacts and resource intensity "throughout the life cycle to a level in line with the earth's carrying capacity". These goals can only be addressed by the firm working with others, including its suppliers, customers and competitors. WBCSD has also emphasised the need for firms to work with governments.

2.1.1. Indicators and targets

Several of the goals in the WBCSD definition of eco-efficiency are difficult to define in measurable terms. Nevertheless, considerable effort has been made by businesses to develop useful indicators, benchmarks and criteria. WBCSD (BCSD, 1993) identifies seven eco-efficiency criteria for firms:

a) minimise the material intensity of goods and services;

b) minimise the energy intensity of goods and services;

c) minimise toxic dispersion;

d) enhance material recyclability;

e) maximise the use of renewable resources;

f) extend product durability;

g) increase the service intensity of goods and services.

Dow Europe uses the pictorial device of the "eco-compass" to represent six different components of eco-efficiency (see Box 2). Other devices, such as histograms and star-rating systems, have been developed for use in eco-labels. Such simple, qualitative indicators are useful for decision-making

---

Box 2

The Eco-Compass

Dow Europe has developed the "eco-compass" to assess potential product innovations against six scales (see below).

An existing product is arbitrarily assigned a score of 2 on each scale. Product innovations are scored relative to the existing product, resulting in a graphic display of their strengths and weaknesses. An ideal product would score 5 on all six objectives, covering the entire surface area of the hexagon.

The eco-compass is used by Dow as part of a creative process to identify more eco-efficient alternatives to existing products and as a communication device. The assignment of scores in each of the six dimensions is often qualitative.

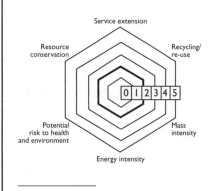

Source: Fussler, 1996.

purposes, especially when searching for products and services that offer large improvements in eco-efficiency.

Attempts have also been made to capture eco-efficiency in a single dimension. This requires a weighting system to add up its several components. A few organisations have developed this kind of weighting approach to rank products or firms according to environmental performance. The Swiss pharmaceutical company Roche has developed an indicator which it calls the "eco-efficiency rate" (EER). Roche calculates EER by dividing the value of total corporate sales by the sum of expenditure on environmental protection and the estimated monetary value of environmental damage caused (DeSimone et al., 1997). There is little prospect for general acceptance of such a standardised indicator, as this would require agreement on the weighting system.

Several companies have set targets for reductions in pollutant release and resource use. For example, DuPont's targets for 2000 include:

– eliminate emissions of CFC, nitrous oxide (N_2O), and airborne carcinogens;

– reduce hazardous air emissions by 50% relative to 1995 level;

– reduce packaging waste by 50% relative to 1991 level;

– reduce hazardous waste by 35% relative to 1995 level;

– reduce aqueous discharges by 25% relative to 1995 level (DuPont, 1997).

Other manufacturing and service sector companies have similar targets. Sectoral targets have been set by industry associations in several countries, as part of their voluntary agreements with governments.

2.1.2. Changes in production processes

Innovation in production processes tends to focus on reducing the use of expensive inputs – in particular labour. Spending on energy and raw materials is a small component of overall costs for most industries, giving little incentive to reduce waste. Nevertheless, several major companies have made efforts to do so. Well-known examples include Dow's "Waste Reduction Always Pays" (WRAP) programme (see Box 3) and 3M's "Pollution Prevention Pays" (3P) programme.

WBCSD and the OECD's Business and Industry Advisory Committee (BIAC) have
collected many other examples of initiatives from companies including Bayer,

DuPont, ICI, and GlaxoWellcome. They include new processes that completely eliminate waste or pollution streams, or that reduce them considerably. The many case studies demonstrate the importance of clear leadership from the company management, reinforced by education and direct involvement of the workforce, who are the source of most innovations. Most existing examples are from large, transnational companies which are able to devote a board member specifically to environmental issues and have well-organised systems for innovation. Engaging the capabilities of staff in small and medium-sized enterprises could greatly increase the probability of achieving industry-wide eco-efficiency improvements.

Box 3

"Waste Reduction Always Pays"

Dow encourages its staff to identify opportunities for waste reduction and pollution prevention. Each manufacturing division is responsible for its own development and implementation of the "Waste Reduction Always Pays Programme" (WRAP).

WRAP initiatives have achieved substantial reductions in emissions and inputs, e.g. 50% reduction in spills at a polyurethane plant; 80% reduction in consumption of a reactant in an agricultural products plant; 93% reduction in air emissions and 48% increase in production capacity at a latex plant.

WRAP projects also save money, and are expected to continue yielding 30-40% returns on capital for the foreseeable future.

Source: DeSimone et al., 1997.

Many improvements in material and energy efficiency pay for themselves in less than a year. Energy efficiency experts typically estimate that energy savings of 10-30% could be made economy-wide through changes in practices and technology that pay for themselves (IPCC, 1996). WBCSD and its member companies emphasise that a shift in taxation from employment to pollution would make larger savings profitable. Experience from 150 manufacturing companies in Poland, representing more than 20 branches of industry, is that 20-40% of waste could be avoided with zero or minor investment. Where investment is required, it usually pays for itself in material savings within a few weeks or months, and external financing is rarely required. A further 30% reduction is possible through investments in technologically proven and profitable equipment or process changes. Similar results have been obtained in other central and eastern European countries (OECD, 1995b). Best practice programmes in the United Kingdom, the United States and elsewhere have yielded comparable results.

Considerable water savings may also be possible. The French Ministry of the Environment (Ministère de l'Environnement, 1997) estimates that good housekeeping in France in 1996 could have reduced water consumption by 15% while saving 65 million francs (about US$10 million).

2.1.3. Product innovations

Numerous innovations have demonstrated the potential to improve the eco-efficiency of products including cars, houses, refrigerators and televisions (von Weizsäcker *et al.*, 1997; DeSimone *et al.*, 1997). Innovations typically succeed in the market if they reduce costs, improve performance, or meet some need that was not addressed by existing products.

Innovations are often used to increase the utility or value of a product without reducing resource use or pollutant release. Hence, eco-efficiency improvements may not lead to reduced environmental impacts without government intervention. Car technology is an obvious example. Fuel intensity (L/100 km) per kilogram of car mass has also declined by about a quarter in standard tests in OECD countries over the last 15 years (IEA, 1997a). A recent development by Mitsubishi to commercialise their "gasoline direct injection" engine enables them to offer further energy savings of 20% or more, at the same time as increasing power output by 10%. Many "concept cars" have been developed by manufacturers and others (including the Greenpeace SMILe) with fuel intensity a third that of the current average. A factor of ten reduction in life-cycle fuel and mass intensity may be technically possible (von Weizsäcker *et al.*, 1997). These reductions in material and energy use are not achieved in practice because, according to manufacturers, the cars would be too expensive or would not meet consumers' needs for driving performance, comfort and safety at low cost. In general, improved efficiency is used to boost performance and increase car size. While cars at the smaller end of the market have become steadily more energy-efficient, consumers are buying bigger cars, so that the average new car bought today consumes no less energy than that bought at the beginning of the 1980s. Much greater progress has been made in managing urban air pollution from cars than in managing energy and material use. Cars built in the mid 1990s produced about one twentieth of the carbon monoxide emissions per kilometre driven of those built in the 1970s. Emissions per kilometre of NO_x and VOC have been reduced about ten-fold. This progress is due primarily to government regulations.

Box 4

The Philips Green Television

Philips, a major television manufacturer, decided in 1993 to build a prototype "Green TV". The prototype was a 14 inch model which achieved:

- *98% reduction in stand-by power (while the TV is waiting to be used);*
- *30% reduction in operating energy;*
- *11% weight reduction;*
- *22% increase in use of recycled materials;*
- *total elimination of toxic substances;*
- *a design that maximised recyclability.*

The prototype did not enter mass production, but many of its features, in particular those that save energy, have been used for models entering the market from 1997.

Source: WBCSD.

Attempts to improve eco-efficiency often fail because they increase the up-front cost to the customer of a product, even if they do not increase costs over the life-cycle. Milani (1997) provides the example of an attempt by the Swiss government to persuade refrigerator manufacturers to use more energy-efficient technology. The technology would pay for itself in electricity savings over several years, but increased the cost of the appliance by a third. Manufacturers did not adopt the design, explaining that the change in technology was too large and that consumers would not buy the refrigerators. This experience contrasts with that of Greenpeace's "GreenFreeze". This refrigerator, developed with a manufacturer in former Eastern Germany, used a hydrocarbon refrigerant instead of the usual CFC substitutes which are strong greenhouse gases. With little or no increase in cost, this refrigerator was a great success and major manufacturers have now introduced models with hydrocarbon refrigerants.

> **Box 5**
>
> ### The paperless office?
>
> Computer technology and telecommunications promised to bring the paperless office, but have so far increased paper consumption by making it easier to produce, modify and print documents. Paper recycling is one way to achieve moderate reductions in the environmental impacts of paper use. Now, researchers at the Massachusetts Institute of Technology (MIT) have developed a product which could allow paper to be re-used up to 100 times. The product is a special kind of ink which is clear until it is activated by heat. Millions of dots of the ink on ordinary paper can be turned black by a device like a laser printer. The dots can be turned clear again by heating to a slightly higher temperature. A colour version of the ink is also available, and can be re-used 1 000 times. MIT has already achieved 300 dots-per-inch resolution with the technology, and is aiming for 600-1 000 dots-per-inch.

Firms have found it technically easier to reduce the use of toxic materials than to reduce energy use. For example, Nortel (Northern Telecom) in Canada introduced the world's first lead-free telephone to the market in 1996, having developed lead-free soldering technology. Philips have built a "Green TV" containing no toxic substances (see Box 4). However, such technologies may only be commercially viable if new government policies are introduced.

WBCSD emphasises product durability as a key element of eco-efficiency. Improved durability will obviously reduce waste in highly consumable products such as paper (see Box 5). Companies are increasingly moving back to re-usable packaging, including returnable bottles. On the other hand, there is no sign of a shift away from the use of disposable paper and plastic products.

The advantages of durability are less obvious in longer-lived products whose environmental impacts occur mainly during use. Cars, refrigerators and buildings

25

are key examples. Where technology is improving rapidly in environmental performance, there may be advantages in scrapping older stock early, especially if components are re-used or recycled.

2.1.4. Changing producer-consumer relationships

Innovations that change the producer-consumer relationship are rare relative to the others discussed above, and may provide more opportunity to reduce the resource impacts of consumption. The concept of "extended and shared producer responsibility" (EPR) is beginning to change the producer-consumer relationship (Vancini, 1997). EPR is sometimes enshrined in law but is also spreading as a business philosophy. Some producers are beginning to address environmental impacts in the up-stream supply of materials and services and the downstream use and disposal of their products. This is partly because they are aware of consumers' growing ability to use their purchasing power to influence the design of products and the provision of services. For many producers, taking responsibility for post-consumer waste can even be profitable. Approaches include:

- **Asset recovery, remanufacturing and recycling**. Xerox introduced an asset recovery programme for its photocopiers in 1987, in which parts of end-of-life machines are recovered for re-use or recycling (see Box 6). As a result of the programme, Xerox has reduced its production of landfill waste from 2 500 to 1 000 tonnes per year. The money saved by the programme was estimated at $69.4 million in 1995. The approach is also used for computers by IBM and Siemens-Nixdorf. Sony has introduced a programme for remanufacturing equipment.

- **Modular design**. This is the key to the approach used by Interface Flooring Systems to reduce carpet waste. Office carpets need frequent replacement, but only 20% of a carpet receives 80% of the wear. By providing tiles instead of broadloom carpets, Interface develops an ongoing service relationship with its customers, replacing worn flooring tiles and recycling the materials from recovered tiles.

- **Moving from products to services**. This approach is given particular empha-

---

> **Box 6**
>
> **Successful asset recovery**
>
> *Many factors can contribute to the success of companies' efforts to provide an innovative service. Smith (1997) attributes the success of Xerox's asset recovery approach to a variety of factors, including:*
>
> - *A well-developed infrastructure to return used photocopiers to the factory.*
> - *Close relationships with customers.*
> - *The robust design of its products.*
> - *Providing a total satisfaction guarantee.*
> - *Committed and visionary management.*

sis by advocates of eco-efficiency. The idea is that companies provide consumers with a service, retaining ownership of, and responsibility for, any equipment. Dow has introduced a "rent-a-chemical" scheme. The concept of selling services rather than products has perhaps been most developed by electric utilities, selling energy services rather than just electricity. Utilities can often afford to invest in energy-efficient equipment with longer payback times than their customers would consider.

Unfortunately, firms that are addressing the full life-cycle of their products and services are in the minority. Government has a key role to play in ensuring that firms are aware of the opportunities for life-cycle management, and have incentives to take them. This government role will be examined in Section 2.6. The next few sections consider eco-efficiency initiatives outside the business sector.

2.2. INITIATIVES IN AGRICULTURE

Strategies for improving eco-efficiency are just as applicable in agriculture as they are in other production sectors. Eco-efficiency improvements in agriculture can come both from radical shifts in farm practices, such as the use of natural predators for pest control, and from the introduction of improved plant and livestock varieties. Kate Fish (1997) of Monsanto gives examples of both genetically engineered plants and modified farm practices that reduce the environmental impacts of agriculture at the same time as cutting costs. Recent controversies over genetic engineering also illustrate the potential for innovations to face challenges in the market place for reasons other than cost and performance.

While changes in production processes could substantially reduce the environmental impacts of food production, retailers also have a key role to play. Some supermarket chains (*e.g.* Sainsbury's in the United Kingdom) have introduced purchasing policies that emphasise reduced chemical inputs and improved land management. However, they do not market their products as "low input", believing that this would not be a good selling point.

2.3. INITIATIVES IN SERVICES

Examples of eco-efficiency improvement are less common in the services sector than in manufacturing industry. This may be partly because the environmental impacts of service provision are less obvious than those of manufacturing. Service companies also tend to be smaller than manufacturers of consumer products, and are less likely to have resources to devote to monitoring and improving their environmental performance. One exception is in telecommunications. Tuppen (1997) offers several examples of eco-efficiency improvements introduced by British Telecom. These include: the introduction of refrigerant-free telephone exchange cooling, which has resulted in a 50% reduction in both energy consumption and capital costs for cooling equipment; efforts to re-use or recycle telephones; and a programme to reduce paper consumption.

Some financial service companies have also made efforts to improve eco-efficiency, both by developing "green" investment portfolios and by examining the environmental impacts of their own operations. For example, ING Group is implementing environmental management systems, reducing energy consumption in its offices, and developing a commuting plan for its staff. ING focuses on staff initiative, which is encouraged through an "eco-label" to recognise teams' environmental achievement. ING is also considering introducing environmental aspects into its system for evaluating staff (Kroon, 1997).

2.4. INITIATIVES IN LOCAL GOVERNMENT

Local governments can adopt strategies to improve the eco-efficiency of their operations in much the same way as other service organisations. Public sector organisations can improve eco-efficiency by paying attention both to the goods and services they produce, and to those they consume. The public sector plays a role in designing and building houses; planning transport services and infrastructure; and providing education, health care and utilities such as water and electricity. Eco-efficiency, cleaner production and pollution prevention principles are beginning to be applied to all of these areas. Public transport operators in many countries use alternative fuels as a result of government policies to develop and experiment with those fuels. There are numerous examples of city, regional and state authorities that have found ways of saving materials and energy or reducing pollution while also saving money and improving the service they provide.

Local governments are also of particular interest as a source of innovation in policy: they can often experiment with measures that could not be applied at a national level. A recent OECD study (OECD, 1997i) identifies a range of examples of community and local government innovation in transport planning and pricing. These include: authorities in Portland, Oregon, and Central Region, Scotland, which have used scenarios as a tool to discuss transport policy options with the public; the cities of Bergen, Oslo and Trondheim in Norway, which have introduced entry charges for vehicles; and cities in Germany that have tried, with very limited success, to develop car-free residential zones.

A large number of local government programmes have been undertaken in the context of the programmes of the International Council for Local Environmental Initiatives (ICLEI). In ICLEI's "Cities for Climate Protection" (CCP) programme, more than 180 cities have made a commitment to reduce their greenhouse gas emissions. ICLEI has established a standard framework for CCP participants in which they:

1. construct a greenhouse gas emission inventory;
2. produce an emission forecast;
3. adopt targets and timetables for emission reductions;
4. adopt a local action plan to achieve the targets;
5. implement the measures.

So far, 62 of the cities have completed all five steps. Many of the targets adopted are more ambitious than the national targets adopted in the Kyoto Protocol to the UN Framework Convention on Climate Change (FCCC). About half of the cities aim to reduce their emissions by 20% over 15 years. The measures they have implemented mostly aim to reduce energy use in buildings and transport, or to reduce methane emissions from waste. These cities report a range of benefits from the measures they have implemented, including improvements in air quality, reduced municipal operating costs, creation of local jobs, improved municipal productivity, reduced traffic congestion and an improved urban environment (ICLEI, 1997).

2.5. STRATEGIES FOR SOCIAL INNOVATION – CHANGING CONSUMPTION PATTERNS

The challenges of sustainable development may require social innovation as much as technical innovation (Lundvall, 1988). As mentioned at the beginning of Section 2, social and technical change are closely linked, especially when the changes are large.

Individuals have to decide for themselves whether a specific change in their consumption patterns leads to improvement or deterioration in their quality of life. Successful innovations may spread and become normal behaviour, but cannot be pre-selected by government experts. The next few paragraphs consider a range of local initiatives in the transport and household sectors. These examples illustrate the use of strategies similar to the WBCSD approach to eco-efficiency, involving identifying indicators, goals and criteria; undertaking a process of change in technology, behaviour and ways of thinking; and monitoring the results.

2.5.1. Eco-efficiency in the transport sector

The OECD commissioned a report in 1996 (ERM, 1996), and held a workshop in 1997 to evaluate the potential for applying "eco-efficiency" to the transport sector. The concept of eco-efficiency clearly applies to vehicles as to other products, and Section 2.1.3 gave some examples of efforts to develop more eco-efficient cars. However, it is more evident in the transport sector than elsewhere that cleaner technology alone will not be sufficient to reverse the rising trend in resource use and environmental damage.

Many public and private sector organisations have sought ways of reducing travel and freight movements, yet continuing to meet consumers' needs. However, there is an ongoing debate about the nature of these needs. While there has recently been a shift in transport policy from targeting "mobility" needs to "access" needs, many travel choices are motivated more by status or other social needs (OECD, 1996c). Current transport patterns have developed in conjunction with settlement patterns, lifestyles, habits, social networks, work and education. The value provided by the transport sector is lodged in a tangle of social and economic values, making it extremely difficult to define the eco-efficiency of transport services in a generally acceptable way. Eco-efficiency indicators *can* be defined but they are controversial and several are likely to be needed.

The dynamic of innovation remains important. In addition to technical change, social and institutional developments could play a major role in transport. Box 7 describes one type of innovation – in the nature of car ownership – which could substantially reduce car use. In a similar way, changes in the organisation of freight transport services, for example through firms pooling loads or contracting out spare vehicle capacity, can reduce truck mileage.

Box 7

Changing behaviour?

Swiss membership of car-sharing schemes has grown exponentially over the last ten years, reaching over 12 000 in 1996 and increasing by about 50-75% per year. Early members were environmentally motivated but more recent members are choosing to car-share for convenience or to save money.

Car sharers drive less than car owners because they do not have a car in their garage or on the doorstep that they can use for short trips. Former car owners who join the system drive less than before (down from 9 000 km per year to 4 000 km per year on average). Those who did not own cars before do not increase their driving (average 1 500 km/year) but no longer borrow or hire cars.

Those joining the system report an improved quality of life, increasing the flexibility of their personal mobility while avoiding the stress of routine driving and car ownership.

Car sharers spend less on car use than car owners. There are so far no detailed studies to show how they use the money they save, or of the associated environmental impacts.

Source: Harms and Truffer, personal communication, 1997.

2.5.2. Household consumption patterns

One attempt to encourage and guide social innovation has been initiated by an international environmental organisation, "Global Action Plan for the Earth" (GAP). In its "EcoTeam Program", GAP works with small community groups to monitor and reduce their resource use and environmental impacts. The programme has a number of environmental goals for its participants by 2000. These are: 65% reduction in household waste; 30% reduction in consumption of electricity, natural gas and water; and 40% reduction in transport energy use. GAP starts from the assumption that many people have attitudes consistent with moving towards environmentally sustainable behaviour, but that they do not have sufficient information to do so, nor do they believe that they alone can make a difference.

The "EcoTeam" is a group of 6 to 10 people who might be neighbours, or acquainted in some other way. They meet once a month and discuss ideas, experiences and achievements related to the EcoTeam programme. The programme is based on a workbook which addresses six areas in turn: waste, gas, electricity, water, transport and consumption. Each team is supported by a coach or by a reporting centre. EcoTeam members work towards changing aspects of household behaviour. They work with other members of their own household to change behaviour in areas such as waste separation and recycling, water use, energy use, and transport.

GAP has set up EcoTeams, and developed Workbooks and support material, in several countries. While GAP monitors the results of its programme, the most detailed evaluation has been carried out in the Netherlands. Six to nine months after the programme, participants have reduced their waste generation by about 40% and electricity consumption by around 30% (Staats and Harland, 1995).

Several other organisations and community groups have made similar efforts, under titles such as "Simplicity Circles", "Voluntary Simplicity" and "Downshifting". More research is needed to evaluate the extent to which participants in these groups succeed in reducing their environmental impacts, and to evaluate the possible economic impacts of widespread replication of their efforts.

2.6. THE ROLE OF NATIONAL GOVERNMENT IN STIMULATING INNOVATION BY FIRMS AND COMMUNITIES

Innovation is essentially a creative or experimental activity. The outcome cannot be controlled or predicted (Nelson, 1982). Participants in an OECD workshop on *Individual Travel Behaviour* (OECD, 1996c) emphasised the role of experimentation in behavioural change, and the same applies to technical change. Sometimes attempts by central governments to stimulate innovation can actually constrain the outcome. In view of the pitfalls of policy in this area, many policy analysts believe that it is best to leave innovation to the market. Indeed, the capitalist economy is one of the most effective systems for innovation (Schumpeter, 1943). On the other hand, there are many ways in which governments can work with the market to increase the rate of innovation and to guide it towards societal goals, if they are well-defined. There are two main economic justifications for government intervention:

- firms and individuals have limited financial incentive to innovate because any new invention can be copied by others, reducing the profits of the innovator. Governments may need to intervene to ensure that the level of innovation effort reflects the social benefits;

- the direction of innovation depends on the priorities of the innovators. They may make inefficient (economically "suboptimal") efforts where their priorities differ systematically from those of society as a whole, or where they have poor information on long-term social needs.

Nelson (1982) draws on a number of industry case studies to show that private firms and individuals probably do make sufficient effort to innovate. He even suggests that, in some sectors, the nature of competition means that firms put too much effort into innovation, trying to be the first to market a new product. On the other hand, he concludes that firms' R&D portfolios are generally much narrower than would be desirable to address societal needs. Firms tend to target their R&D on local, short-term objectives and the outcome can have lasting and pervasive effects on technology development. This phenomenon is known as "lock-in". Rosenberg (1994) describes how resource-intensive but labour-saving technology for manufacturing agricultural tools was developed first to meet local conditions in North America. Initially, this type of technology was not able to compete with traditional techniques in resource-poor, labour-rich Europe, but as a result of efficiency improvements and superior product quality it became competitive.

Section 3 considers a range of policies that have systemic effects on the pricing and regulatory incentives that guide innovative efforts by firms and others. However, there may still be a need for policies to stimulate innovation in specific sectors or for specific purposes. A major challenge for governments is to develop a view of the types of technology that might be needed in the long term for sustainable development, and to create local conditions that will stimulate the development of that technology. This section identifies some of the approaches that have been taken in OECD Member countries.

One of the main lessons from past experience of government efforts to stimulate innovation is that there are no simple rules for policy design. Appropriate policies vary, depending on the characteristics of the particular sector and the government's objectives in that sector (Nelson, 1982). It is difficult for governments to strike the right balance in their relationship to innovators. On the one hand, governments can develop intelligent policies only where they develop a good understanding of the needs of innovators in industry, local government and other institutions (Wallace, 1995). On the other hand, some distance is needed to avoid government officials being constrained by the prevalent assumptions of those organisations.

2.6.1. Supporting the development of indicators and goals

Many OECD governments work with individual companies or with sector organisations to develop voluntary targets for environmental improvement. Many of these agreements target regulated pollutants or greenhouse gases. Usually, the targets are expressed in terms of emission reductions per unit of physical output. That is, they are targets for eco-efficiency improvements rather than absolute environmental improvements.

There is a need for more open dialogue between industry and government to determine which indicators and criteria are useful and feasible. Such a dialogue has begun in Canada, where the National Round Table on the Environment and the Economy is developing a shared view on the choice of indicators for eco-efficiency (see Box 8). NRTEE has found that, while material and energy intensity goals are feasible and relevant to sustainable development, goals for service intensity and durability are less relevant.

2.6.2. Promoting R&D, discovery and information exchange

Research, development and demonstration policy has made a transition in recent years in many OECD coun-

---

Box 8

Indicators of Eco-Efficiency

Canada's National Round Table on the Environment and the Economy brings together industry and government representatives to develop a common understanding of environmental issues. They are examining indicators of eco-efficiency, and have so far concluded that:

Indicators for reduction of material intensity and energy intensity are readily measurable, but should be measured separately.

Indicators for reduction of toxic dispersion are highly desirable and relatively feasible. Further work is required to examine existing practices and requirements for reporting toxic releases and comparing the toxicity of different substances.

Indicators of material recyclability, use of renewable resources and product durability could easily be developed, but further consideration is needed on the best choice of indicators.

Indicators for service intensity and product life-time cost will be more difficult to design and implement.

Source: NRTEE, 1997.

tries. In the 1960s and 1970s, much R&D was carried out in universities or in government laboratories, with government funding and sometimes government oversight. At the same time, firms carried out their own R&D which might interface with university programmes at conferences and through literature, but projects were rarely collaborative.

More recently, several factors, including tight budgets, have led to a much closer integration of the research programmes of governments and private companies. Policies focus increasingly on facilitating the exchange of ideas among firms, and among different types of institution. Japan has been a leader in this style of research and product development, with very close co-operation between government and private industry. In the European Union, research carried out with European Commission support usually involves several partners, including universities and companies from different Member countries. In the United States, the Partnership for a New Generation of Vehicles (PNGV) is one example of the collaborative efforts that have emerged.

A further important feature in recent years has been the increased focus on results – many related to improving eco-efficiency – in government R&D programmes. PNGV aims to develop new technology that meets a particular set of objectives for energy efficiency and pollution reduction. Targets and milestones are also an important feature of R&D programmes in Japan, the European Union and elsewhere.

Most R&D co-operation has focused on developing technology that is far from commercialisation. This means that it is hard to judge the outcome of the research as it rarely leads to a visible product. Nevertheless, R&D co-operation is a valuable opportunity for firms to develop networks and exchange ideas. Firms are less enthusiastic about co-operating as they approach commercialisation of a technology because they would lose the profits resulting from the innovation. Governments can encourage near-market R&D via the patent system. A long patent life, combined with strong enforcement of intellectual property rights and simple, low-cost procedures for patent application, can enhance the incentive to innovate. However, a balance has to be struck between promoting innovation and encouraging diffusion, which is inhibited by strong patent laws.

2.6.3. Developing niche markets

Government and public sector procurement and planning policies often create niche markets to encourage early application of new technology. The challenge for governments is to take a strategic approach, ensuring that users have the opportunity to choose the innovations that best meet their needs in the long term and reject those that do not. It is very difficult to know when to phase out support, and to make sure that suppliers have sufficient incentive to reduce costs. Governments have been criticised for maintaining support for technology that was clearly uneconomic in areas including alternative fuels and supersonic civil aviation. However, criticism is often more vocal when governments withdraw support from uneconomic projects.

The United Kingdom's Non-Fossil Fuel Obligation (NFFO) system for renewable energy has been one successful way of creating niche markets for near-commercial technology. NFFO involves periodic calls for tender to supply electricity to the UK national grid from various categories of renewable energy source. There are clear limits both in the size of the market to be supported and the time for which the support will last. Companies that succeed in the tendering process can sell electricity to the grid at the price they bid. In successive rounds of NFFO since 1990, the costs of several renewable energy sources have fallen in the United Kingdom.

"Green procurement" is one of the most promising approaches to generating niche markets for clean technology. The United States Environmental Protection Agency's Energy Star programme has become world famous by effectively setting the standard for energy-efficient computers.

2.6.4. Addressing communication gaps

Once new technologies and practices have succeeded in niche markets, their further use depends on other potential users hearing about them. Most of the well-known companies with eco-efficiency programmes are large multinationals and leaders in their fields, with strong internal systems for innovation.

Whereas large companies often have the internal machinery to monitor and adopt best practice in their industry, governments may have a particular role to play in relation to small and medium-sized enterprises (SMEs) and the service sector. In Portugal, the government has worked with SMEs to achieve substantial progress in reducing energy and material waste and environmental impacts (see Box 9). The Australian government is working with public sector organisations to improve their environmental performance – for example, by producing a "Green Health Guide" for hospitals.

SMEs tend to be less able to introduce new technology and product innovations than large companies partly because of their limited access to information. Smaller companies and the service sector in general may also be less able to market new products than large manufacturers.

Box 9

Targeting small and medium-sized enterprises in Portugal

The Portuguese Institute for Environmental Technology (ITA) has implemented a programme for cleaner production, targeting small and medium-sized enterprises (SMEs). In one glass company the programme resulted in an investment of 89 million Escudos which tripled output while improving by-product use and reducing production of waste water, sludge, and CO_2. The company has saved 200 million Escudos.

ITA has identified several keys to improving eco-efficiency:

- *education of workforces;*
- *helping SMEs to identify areas for technology development;*
- *creative co-operation between the ITA team and company representatives;*
- *social and financial incentives to stimulate consumer preferences and reward companies for environmentally improved products and services;*
- *addressing multiple eco-efficiency objectives, such as energy and material efficiency, together.*

Source: Peneda, 1997.

Communication gaps on environmental issues are shrinking, partly thanks to government initiatives, but more importantly because of new communication technology and business initiatives. Businesses increasingly recognise the need to address sustainable development as a result of the efforts of organisations such as Keidanren in Japan and the National Round Table for the Environment and the Economy in Canada, as well as WBCSD and the regional business councils for sustainable development. Meanwhile, large companies' need to manage the environmental impacts of their products throughout the life-cycle is increasingly leading them to ask for environmental management assurances from their SME suppliers.

2.6.5. Facilitating social innovation

Policy discussion on innovation has traditionally focused on technology R&D. However, the OECD's work has highlighted the need for the social and behavioural sciences to play a role in developing policy that affects lifestyles, institutions and technologies (OECD, 1997e). As in the case of technological innovation, some of the most effective policies to encourage social innovation may be those that provide a more general economic, legal and physical framework. These are discussed in the next section.

Local governments, other local organisations and community leaders can be effective in informing consumers and encouraging them to change their purchasing patterns. Environment Australia (1996) has collected a number of case studies of local governments that have successfully addressed local environmental problems. For example, Albury City Council undertook a community awareness programme to reduce phosphorus discharges, persuading citizens to switch to zero and low-phosphorus washing powders and change their car washing habits. OECD (1997i) provides examples of stakeholder processes that have led to changes in local transport planning. Central governments can facilitate such changes. The United States' Intermodal Surface Transportation Efficiency Act (ISTEA) of 1991 emphasises involving stakeholders as a first step for Metropolitan Planning Organisations in developing their transport plans (see Box 10). ISTEA has led to a rapid increase in investment in cycling, pedestrian and public transport schemes (Kienitz, 1997).

A recent OECD study identified several government programmes to encourage stakeholder consultation processes through transport planning guidelines for local governments (OECD, 1997i).

The study found that:

- national efforts, such as that in the United States, succeed mainly in regions where there is already strong interest in community participation and where local expertise is available;

- achieving the full involvement of a local community in decision-making is very demanding in time and effort; but

---

Box 10

ISTEA:
A framework for innovation

The US Inter-modal Surface Transportation Efficiency Act of 1991 (ISTEA) requires States and Metropolitan Planning Organisations (MPOs) to improve co-ordination, develop procedures for community involvement in decision making, and address environmental and social objectives. It also requires them to consider options such as land-use planning.

While the quality of ISTEA implementation varies among MPOs, the Act has led to funding of a wide range of new initiatives including:

- **cycle and pedestrian programmes** *in many cities*

- **congestion pricing projects** *in Seattle and at the Maine Turnpike, as well as an educational project on congestion pricing in Portland, Oregon and a toll on the San Francisco-Oakland Bay bridge*

- **innovative transit projects** *including a segregated busway in Miami, an information system for Denver's bus system, an alternative fuel bus fleet in Boise, Idaho, and electric shuttle buses in Chattanooga, Tennessee*

- **intermodal freight and transit projects** *including intermodal freight terminals in Maine and Stark County, and an intermodal passenger terminal in Worcester, Massachusetts.*

- the consultation process can lead to a change in the preferences of local communities and can increase support for policies once they are adopted.

Governments can and do also use broad-based incentives to encourage changes in behaviour, institutions and local government practices. Measures such as land-use planning may be essential in moving towards sustainable cities, but are usually managed at a local level. Policies often used by central governments include taxes and tax rebates; links between local government funding and the achievement of environmental practices; and monitoring and support for demonstration projects.

The likelihood of success and potential for replication of an innovation depend partly on the degree of technical and social change required. Many factors in the technical, economic and social environment are also important (Smith *et al.*, 1997) and are discussed in Section 3. Government policies form a key element of this environment. Important policies include safety standards and other regulations, taxes, subsidies and other market instruments. Governments also play a role in the more general cultural and institutional framework that influences the success and replication of any innovation.

2.6.6. Monitoring and feedback

Feedback is an essential component of a strategy to improve eco-efficiency, serving both to monitor trends and to evaluate the effectiveness of action that has been taken. Several OECD governments offer awards for good practice in environmental reporting and support for developing environmental management systems (EMS). The ISO 14000 Series now provides an international basis for the development of EMS. Common standards for life-cycle analysis (ISO 14040) provide a framework for co-operation along the production chain and have been effective in involving SMEs in improving eco-efficiency.

Company and sector monitoring contributes to national monitoring, but also plays a role at the company level. Once companies start to record their use and wastage of energy and materials, and their emissions of pollutants, they usually begin to reduce them. Thus, "monitoring and targeting" schemes have played a key role in many governments' industrial energy efficiency strategies over the last two decades.

Public reporting can sometimes provide a stronger incentive than regulations for organisations to manage their environmental impacts. UNEP (1994) recommends a set of 50 "ingredients" that should be included in company environmental reports, and a core set of 20 ingredients for reporting by SMEs. These ingredients cover management policies and systems; inventories of environmental impacts; financial implications of environmental actions; relationships with environmental stakeholders; and broader sustainable development issues.

OECD has been working with Member countries to develop a methodology for producing pollution release and transfer registers (OECD, 1996*b*). Pollutant Release and Transfer Register data indicate the amount of specific pollutants being released or transferred by a facility. The data can be used to determine pollution per unit of product or to show progress in a firm's efforts to reduce pollution.

3. IMPROVING ECO-EFFICIENCY THROUGHOUT THE ECONOMY

This section moves from the perspective of individual innovations to that of the economy as a whole. It opens by reviewing aggregate indicators and targets for eco-efficiency. It continues by identifying conditions that influence the rate of resource productivity improvement, and concludes by discussing ways in which governments can help to improve eco-efficiency economy-wide. These include developing national goals, indicators and criteria for eco-efficiency improvement; introducing policies to encourage and orient innovation towards the goals; and establishing systems to monitor the effects of those policies.

3.1. NATIONAL ECO-EFFICIENCY INDICATORS

While governments can and do make use of many of the principles of the WBCSD approach to eco-efficiency, they are likely to need different types of goals and indicators from those used by firms, reflecting the societal scale at which they operate. For example, whereas firms might be interested in the energy intensity of their products and services, governments have long monitored the energy intensity of their national GDP.

Productivity indicators and targets are useful at the national level to orient action by governments. They can help to indicate the kind of change that is needed or desired in order to move towards sustainable development. In general, however, government policies are best aimed at improving the state of the environment, the health of the economy and the quality of life, rather than increasing productivity *per se*. Where efficiency improvements alone are sought, there is a risk that increases in economic activity will outweigh any reduction in environmental impact per unit of activity.

Most productivity analysis is necessarily based on standardised physical or monetary output indicators, such as the volume of goods produced or their value added. At national level, the most common indicator is GDP. Obviously, these indicators cannot capture the full complexity of societal goals.

The WBCSD explanation of eco-efficiency points towards the need to consider "quality of life" and "human needs" in addition to conventional economic indicators. Government policy takes account of "headline" indicators such as the unemployment rate, the number of homeless people, the consumer price index, the trade balance and many others. Quality of life also depends on factors such as time spent with families and community involvement (Merck Family Fund, 1995).

Clearly, many other indicators are needed to capture the "quality of life". Table 1 lists a few examples of indicators that might be readily available. The table also differentiates among economic indicators of "welfare", indicators of the extent to which basic physiological and community needs are met, and indicators of individuals' ability to pursue "higher" needs, which might include intellectual and spiritual development. Indicators of the latter, in particular, are relatively under-developed and controversial.

Table 1. **Examples of eco-efficiency "output" indicators at the national level**

Economic indicators of welfare	Satisfying basic needs	Satisfying higher needs
GDP National accounts based on shadow prices including "green GDP" Income distribution Consumer surplus	UN's Human Development Index (based on income, education and life expectancy) Net migration Share of income spent on basic needs	Average leisure hours Number of books published Number of university graduates Access to advanced communication technology (e.g. Internet connections)

Many attempts have been made to construct single indicators of quality of life, and the extent to which human needs are met. Perhaps the best known of these is the Human Development Index (HDI) developed by the United Nations Development Programme (UNDP, 1997), based on national life expectancy at birth, years of schooling, adult literacy and purchasing power.

Statistics are available for most OECD countries on national emissions of several greenhouse gases, sulphur dioxide, NO_x, and other pollutants (OECD, 1997f). Figures are also available on fresh water use, waste generation, land-use patterns, agricultural inputs, and use of energy and other commodities.

While environmental *pressure* indicators form the denominator or input side of eco-efficiency, *state* of the environment indicators are also important at the national level for defining goals for sustainability. Table 2 gives examples of each of these two types.

emissions, such as sulphur dioxide, are expected to decline in OECD coun
Sulphur emissions in non-OECD countries are projected to increase substan
before being brought under control some time in the next century (see Figure

In 1994, CO_2 projections such as those in Figure 3 led the "Factor 10 Clul
group of 16 prominent environmental experts, to issue the "Carnoules Declarati
In it, they called for a ten-fold improvement in material and energy productivit
industrialised countries over the next 30 to 50 years. They say that this would h.
total resource use while allowing for a doubling of world-wide economic activity
an improvement in international equity. The aim of halving resource use is explai
mainly with reference to greenhouse gas emissions: a halving of CO_2 emissions
2040 would be consistent with a longer term aim of stabilising atmospheric (
concentrations at 350-450 ppm (IPCC, 1997).

Given the divergent trends in environmental pressure shown in Figure 2
does not make sense to adopt a single global efficiency target for all activities a
environmental impacts, even if such a target were considered appropriate for C
from fossil fuel combustion. In some cases, a factor of ten reduction may be mc
than is required for sustainability, and in other cases, less. Meanwhile, environme
tal challenges vary among countries and locations. National efforts are needed
establish sustainable development goals and indicators, suiting specific concerr
No target or set of targets is likely to be universally acceptable because any sol
tion will bring winners and losers. Nor is there any "right" target for the reduction
any specific environmental pressure. Governments, scientists and economists hav
conducted lengthy discussions on targets for greenhouse gas concentrations in tl
atmosphere in the context of the Intergovernmental Panel on Climate Change (IPCC
They have concluded that this is a political, rather than scientific or economic que
tion, although it needs to be informed by both science and economics.

3.3. EXAMPLES OF RECENT CHANGES IN ECO-EFFICIENCY

Local and national circumstances, in particular relative factor prices, help t
shape the rate and direction of technological development. Table 3 summarise:
productivity increases that have been achieved in a range of economies and sector
at different times.

The higher rates of productivity increase in this table are associated with a
variety of influences: competitive pressures; strong price or regulatory incentives
catching up or recovery; or a good "climate for innovation". Mostly, the circumstances
for rapid change do not last long, although some sectors have sustained very fast
improvements over considerable periods.

Table 2. **Examples of eco-efficiency "input" indicators at the national level**

Pressures on the environment	State of the environment
Emissions of pollutants from different types of source (mobile, stationary, sector breakdown)	Remaining mineral resources
	Concentration of pollutants in air, water, biota
Consumption of coal, oil, gas, minerals	Land used for industry or agriculture
Consumption of renewable resources (biomass products, land, fresh water)	Indicators of biodiversity, e.g. number of species
	Ecological footprint (land required to supply national needs on a renewable basis)
Economic valuation of environmental damage	
Use of environmental "services"	Environmental "capital"

Some analysts have suggested that governments should focus on specific types of indicator, which they believe to be good proxies for the many dimensions of eco-efficiency. One such indicator is the "total material requirement" (TMR) of an economy, which is an estimate of the total mass of materials disrupted each year by economic activities (WRI, 1997). Some advocates of TMR as an indicator describe the ratio GDP/TMR as "eco-efficiency". They argue that TMR includes, or is correlated with, a wide range of environmental impacts, ranging from soil erosion to the release of toxic compounds. However, such indicators are not useful for examining long-term trends, nor for giving a full impression of the trends in, and causes of, specific environmental pressures, or for making comparisons between countries.

Other attempts have been made to identify a simple indicator of environmental pressure based on concepts including "ecological footprints" and "environmental space" (OECD, 1997a). Economic techniques can also be used to estimate the cost associated with environmental pressure. Contingent valuation is one approach, involving surveys to establish how much individuals would be prepared to pay to avoid specific environmental impacts. This technique allows for citizens' subjective weighting of different environmental impacts. It can be used to develop composite indicators such as "green GDP" and "natural capital". However, underlying each of these concepts lies a much more complex picture which can be revealed only by using a range of more transparent indicators of specific environmental pressures (World Bank, 1997).

It would be premature to suggest a set of standard indicators at this stage. Governments are just beginning to develop indicator series for their reports on progress towards sustainable development. Measurement and reporting systems may need to evolve over time. Preferred indicators are likely to depend on national circumstances and aims.

3.2. TRENDS AND TARGETS

Many indicators of the output (or nominator) part of the eco-efficiency ratio are improving in OECD countries. OECD residents continue to enjoy growing income and increasing life expectancy. They are spending more time in education and less at work. They are using their rising income to increase their ownership of cars, household appliances and other goods (OECD, 1996a). They are able to travel and communicate more easily and cheaply than ever before.

◆ Figure 2. **OECD trends in GDP and a range of eco-efficiency "input" indicators**
Average annual percentage change, 1985-1995

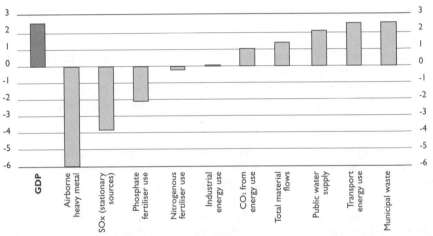

Note: Figures relate to all OECD Member countries except: airborne heavy metals and total material flows, which are fo
  Germany, Japan and United States only; public water supply is for Canada, France, Germany, Japan, United Kingdom and Unite
  States only, 1985-1990.
Sources: OECD Statistics, World Resources Institute.

As Figure 2 shows, some indicators of input (or denominator) part of the eco-efficiency ratio, such as emissions of regulated pollutants, are improving too. The figures for SO_x and heavy metal emissions demonstrate that there is an existin mechanism for resource use and pollutant release to become "decoupled" fror economic activity. As incomes rise, citizens become more willing to vote and some times to pay for a better environment, leading governments to act. Environmenta policies have brought certain types of pollution under control, especially those wit well-proven health effects within national boundaries.

While regulations and other measures have brought some types of pollutio under control, solutions remain to be found for many environmental problems. I particular, as the locus of pollution shifts from local, to national, to regional, to global, solutions become harder to find. There is less incentive to act where environmental damage is remote in time and space, where the impacts are diffuse or not obvious to citizens, or where the response would require a large change in technology or behaviour. Globally, some of the most difficult problems are CO_2 emissions from energy use, and the loss of habitats and biodiversity. At the national and local level, major concerns include the continuing release of toxic chemicals and the disposal of solid waste.

OECD projections show that world GDP could grow to 2.5 times its 1995 level in 2020, with the OECD share falling from 56% in 1995 to between 33% and 44% in 2020 (OECD, 1997*g*). OECD's share of world population is also likely to decline. As non-OECD countries account for a growing share of production and consumption, their exposure and contribution to environmental problems will increase.

Most long-term scenarios see energy use and associated CO_2 emissions by the current OECD countries stabilising from around 2015, although global emissions will go on growing rapidly (OECD, 1997*g*; UNEP, 1997; IPCC, 1995). Globally, deforestation and the depletion of fish stocks are also likely to continue, whereas regulated

◆ Figure 3. **Projected carbon dioxide and sulphur dioxide emissions from fossil fuel combustion, 1980 to 2100, IPCC IS92a Scenario**

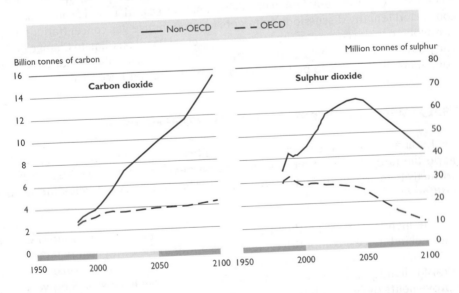

Source: IPCC.

Table 3. **Historical increases in a range of productivity indicators**

Sector/technology	Region	Productivity indicator	Period	Annual productivity change (%)
Whole economy[a]	16 OECD countries	GDP/hours work	1820-1992	+2.4
Whole economy[a]	Japan	GDP/hours work	1950-1973	+7.7
Whole economy[b]	OECD	GDP/primary energy	1971-1995	+1.27
Whole economy[c]	Japan	GDP/material use	1975-1994	+2.0
Whole economy[c]	USA	GDP/material use	1975-1994	+2.5
Whole economy[b]	OECD	GDP/municipal waste	1980-1992	−0.5
Whole economy[b]	6 major OECD countries	GDP/municipal water use	1980-1990	+1.0
Whole economy[b]	Germany, USA	GDP/VOC emissions	1980-1993	+4.0
Whole economy[f]	Germany, Japan, USA	GDP/ heavy metal emissions to air	1965-1995	+7 to +10
Industry[b]	OECD	Industrial production/ energy	1971-1995	+2.5
Industry[b]	OECD	Industrial production/ oil use	1974-1986	+8.0
New cars/light trucks[c]	USA	Vehicle fuel economy	1972-1982	+7.0
New cars/light trucks[c]	USA	Vehicle fuel economy	1982-1992	+0.0
Commercial aviation[d]	World	Tonne-km/energy	1974-1988	+3.8
Commercial aviation[d]	World	Tonne-km/energy	1988-1995	+0.3
Commercial aviation[d]	World	Tonne-km/labour	1974-1995	+5.6
Telephone cables[g]	Transatlantic	Telephone calls/mass	1914-1994	+25.0

Sources: a) Maddison, 1995; b) OECD and IEA statistics; c) Schipper, personal communication 1996; d) ICAO statistics; e) WRI, 1997; f) OECD, 1995a; g) Tuppen, 1997.

These examples do not help us to predict exactly what rate of improvement in eco-efficiency might be possible but they help to identify some challenges for governments. Obvious areas for action include: reforming government policies that limit competition in resource-intensive industries; removing subsidies and tax disincentives; and internalising externalities. Unfortunately, this is not an easy recipe. The more rapid rates of change in Table 3 have occurred only in response to very strong price signals: nominal aviation fuel prices increased nearly ten-fold between 1970 and 1980. Nominal crude oil prices increased by a factor of 30 in the same period while real prices rose ten-fold. It is not surprising, then, that the aviation industry and industry in general made huge efforts to reduce their oil consumption, effectively "decoupling" CO_2 emissions from economic activity. Responses to price changes can also be very complex, depending on the circumstances of any change.

Experience with rapid "catching-up", for example in Japan during the 1950s and 1960s, can help to give some insight into the potential for whole sectors or economies to move towards "best practice". The Japanese experience is often used as a model for creating a "climate for innovation" (e.g., Freeman, 1987; Rosenberg, 1994; Wallace, 1995).

Another observation from Table 3 is that economy-wide changes are much slower than changes in industrial sectors. A key challenge for policies to promote sustainable development is to achieve more rapid change in consumption patterns.

3.4. ECONOMY-WIDE BARRIERS TO CHANGE

Attempts to improve eco-efficiency face several economy-wide barriers. The best recognised of these are market and intervention failures and inefficiencies, which have been extensively analysed by the OECD. Less understood but equally important is "lock-in" to existing technologies and practices, associated with the investment costs and social inertia that can inhibit change. These two types of barrier are considered here, reflecting discussions in the OECD Eco-Efficiency Workshop (Annex III). The lack of access to information or education of individuals throughout the economy is also often described as a "barrier". It is not discussed as such here, but options to improve education are mentioned in Section 3.5.6.

3.4.1. Intervention and market failures

Several OECD workshop participants mentioned the innovation-stifling effects of government subsidies and other policies that support or protect polluting activities, referring to recent studies by the Earth Council (de Moor and Calamai, 1996) and the OECD (1997*b*). Subsidy reform, green tax reform, and the creation of futures markets in environmental goods were discussed as important parts of the dynamic for improving eco-efficiency. The relative costs to businesses of staff, capital, energy, materials and environmental services are among the most important influences on the direction of innovation. For most companies, salaries and wages are the largest expenditure. This cost is amplified by taxes and social security payments. Energy and materials tend to be the smallest items of expenditure and are sometimes subsidised even though their production and use have negative externalities. Shifting the balance of taxation from labour to pollution and resource use would provide an economy-wide incentive to improve eco-efficiency.

3.4.2. "Lock-in"

The phenomenon of technological, behavioural and institutional "lock-in" makes any change look costly, even where changes would bring large economic benefits (Jaeger, 1997). Large changes do occur, but their timing is unpredictable and they are hard to manage. A large organisational change has occurred in recent years in newly deregulated industries, such as airlines and electricity companies. The gasoline engine is an example of a technology that has so far survived all attempts to replace it. Since car manufacturers opted for the Otto-cycle engine at the beginning of this century, a massive infrastructure has been installed for manufacturing engines and supplying fuel. The low cost and high performance resulting from "learning-by-doing" and economies of scale make it extremely hard for any new technology ever to enter the market. Some analysts (e.g. DeLuchi, 1992; MacKenzie, 1994) claim that electric battery or fuel cell technology can compete with the gasoline engine in the near future, if produced in large enough volumes. However, no firm is yet prepared to take the risk of investing in the necessary production capacity. Lovins et al. (1993) believe that an organisational change in the car industry is inevitable: with the current trend towards an increasing diversity of products with lower design and tooling costs, economies of scale will disappear allowing small, new manufacturers with novel technology to enter the market.

Rapid changes already occurring in society may provide opportunities for improving eco-efficiency. The changes include the increasing pervasiveness of "high technology", with the development of communication and information technology, the emergence of biotechnology and other scientific and commercial breakthroughs. Markets and styles of management and organisation are also changing. Collectively, these trends have been described as a move towards a "knowledge-based" economy.

An economy-wide move towards improved eco-efficiency would probably involve the disappearance of some products and firms, and the emergence of new ones. This is an important part of the cost of change. The fear of losing can lead to a culture that discourages change. This culture is strengthened by formal and informal links among governments, businesses and the media. Changing the status quo is likely to involve governments re-examining some of these links and opening up new channels of communication with stakeholders who represent a wider range of interests.

3.5. THE ROLE OF NATIONAL GOVERNMENT IN PROMOTING ECO-EFFICIENCY ECONOMY-WIDE

Rapid economy-wide improvements in eco-efficiency are likely to depend on there being a wide range of influences acting in the same direction. Establishing shared goals and co-ordinating policies among the various government ministries and other public agencies concerned can be a major step towards achieving such synergy .

In many governments, transport, energy and industry ministries view environment policy as a problem rather than a set of shared objectives, despite considerable efforts to design integrated policies. Some governments are beginning to succeed in integrating environmental, economic and sectoral policies: four ministries in the Netherlands have produced a joint policy document on their strategy for sustainable development; several countries' national communications under the UN FCCC represent the result of intensive inter-ministerial efforts to agree on policies. The most successful approaches are those that involve contacts at all levels in the various ministries, and where civil servants have to work on a shared task over an extended period.

Box 11

Backcasting

The Swedish Environmentally Sustainable Transport project involved a group of eleven agencies, including government agencies, industry bodies and research institutions. The group co-operated during 1994-1996 to develop a vision of "environmentally sustainable transport" and a strategy to achieve it (SEPA, 1996). The aim was to define the national environmental goals to be achieved over 25-30 years, i.e. by 2020. The group found that it was relatively easy to envision meeting 50-80% reduction goals for hazardous air pollutants by 2020. They find it harder to identify means of reducing CO_2 emissions and noise exposure rapidly. In particular, a longer term objective for CO_2 was adopted, aiming for a 60% reduction by 2050.

The Rio Declaration (UNCED, 1992) emphasised the need to involve citizens in decision-making, and new media such as the Internet can help. OECD Member countries are increasingly turning to public and stakeholder consultation to develop indicators and goals that are generally accepted. Public acceptance of goals is a first step towards acceptance of the policies that might be needed to reach them.

Some OECD countries have adopted the approach of "backcasting" (see Box 11), applied in the OECD project on *Environmentally Sustainable Transport* (EST). This collective process aims to develop a shared vision of a "sustainable" future and a strategy to achieve it. Such target-led policy-making processes have largely been pioneered in the Netherlands and Scandinavia.

This section addresses ways in which governments can help to create the conditions for improving eco-efficiency and to remove the barriers by intervening in the economic, regulatory, physical and informational environment. Government policies routinely affect markets by ensuring or restricting competition and market access; through fiscal and regulatory measures; and by defining property rights and liabilities. Physical infrastructure, which has a pervasive influence on production and consumption patterns, is usually regulated and sometimes provided by government. Information and education are largely provided by private or locally managed institutions, making this the hardest area for governments to have a substantial influence.

3.5.1. Subsidy and regulatory reform

Many reports have pointed to government subsidies as a major impediment to cleaner production of energy (Greenpeace, 1997; de Moor and Calamai, 1996; Roodman, 1996; Larsen and Shah, 1992; Burniaux *et al.*, 1992). In addition to direct subsidies, governments use a wide variety of measures to support domestic or regional industries, or to protect legal monopolies. These policies inhibit innovation and can lead to higher levels of pollution or resource intensity than would occur in a less constrained market. A recent OECD project investigated subsidy and regulatory reform in considerable detail (OECD, 1997*b*). A set of case studies from industrialised countries shows that reforming supports to coal, electricity and transport could substantially reduce CO_2 and acid gas emissions in some countries. In other countries, subsidy reform would have minimal direct environmental benefits but would increase the effectiveness or reduce the cost of environmental policies such as eco-taxes and emission limits. The social, economic and environmental outcome of reforms depends heavily on specific national and local circumstances, and on the way the reforms are implemented. Direct subsidies are often linked to other forms of support to polluting activities, all of which would need to be reformed to achieve large reductions in pollution. Meanwhile, these support systems usually exist to assist particular groups of people in society, or to protect some perceived national interest. Reform is likely to require extensive consultation, and financial or other aid may be necessary during the transition period.

3.5.2. Eco-taxes

Eco-taxes can alter the reward structure throughout the economy, encouraging innovations that reduce externalities and discouraging those that increase externalities. The OECD has long advocated that fiscal and environmental policies should be made mutually reinforcing (OECD, 1993). This recommendation was reiterated in a report presented to the OECD Council in 1997 (OECD, 1997*c*). Ongoing structural and regulatory

---

Box 12

Experience with eco-taxes

Sweden introduced a sulphur tax in 1991 to stimulate SO_x abatement beyond levels achieved by existing regulation.The result was a reduction in the sulphur content of fuel oils by almost 40% beyond legal standards.

A CO_2 tax in Norway is estimated to have reduced CO_2 emissions from stationary sources by up to 21%.

Tax differentiation between leaded and unleaded gasoline has led to a large reduction in the use of leaded gasoline in many OECD countries.

In Denmark, a tax on non-hazardous waste has doubled the cost of waste dumping and incineration. Between 1985 and 1995, the share of waste dumping in overall waste treatment decreased from 39 to 18% and the rate of reuse and recycling increased from 35 to 61%.

Source: OECD, 1997*c*.

changes in OECD economies provide a context for reassessing fiscal systems. Some governments are adjusting taxes to reflect environmental and other priorities more closely (see Box 12). The effectiveness of environmental taxes in reducing pollution increases when disincentives such as energy subsidies are removed (OECD, 1997*b*).

Figure 4 shows the relationship between gasoline price and consumption in OECD Member countries. Price and income differences explain much, although not all, of the variation in gasoline consumption, and differences in price are largely explained by differences in taxation. It is sometimes argued that taxes on household consumption of energy are regressive. Such regressive effects can be avoided by reducing other taxes or increasing transfers for low-income households.

◆   Figure 4.   ***Gasoline price vs. demand per unit of GDP in OECD countries, 1994***
(Prices and GDP in US$ on purchasing power parity basis)

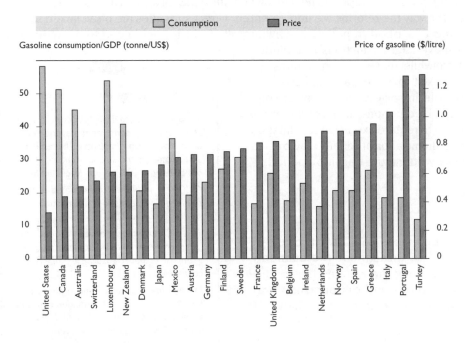

Source: IEA Statistics.

Most OECD governments that have introduced carbon taxes have exempted energy-intensive industry, where they would have the greatest effect, to avoid harming its competitiveness (Baron, 1997). Similarly, while many toll systems are in place for motorways, bridges and tunnels, no national government has introduced a widespread system of road-pricing in urban areas, where most of the externalities of road use occur (OECD, 1997*b*).

Although national governments have relatively little experience with eco-taxes, there has been more ambitious experimentation at the local level. Some state electricity regulators in the United States require utilities to use shadow prices for decisions on investment and plant operation. As mentioned in Section 2.4, numerous cities have experimented with road pricing, or use parking charges to help manage traffic levels. Internalisation may be easier at the local level because opposing lobbies are less well organised, but also because the external costs being addressed are local.

3.5.3. Rights and liabilities

Establishing liability is a vital step towards avoiding environmental damage. Liability for environmental damage is fundamental to the Polluter Pays Principle, whose application has long been recommended by the OECD (1972; 1974; 1975). Similarly, responsibility for the management of materials can be established in law. The OECD has identified the concept of "extended producer responsibility" as a particularly valuable tool to apply the innovative capabilities of businesses to consumption patterns (Vancini, 1997). *Producer* responsibility for environmental impacts *during and after use* of a product is one step towards a broader recognition of the responsibility of all actors throughout a product's life-cycle. Suppliers of goods and services are often able to manage life-cycle impacts more cost-effectively than consumers or the government, while passing part of the cost of life-cycle management on to the consumer.

Experience in the Netherlands has shown that government legislation establishing extended producer responsibility can be highly effective in bringing about technical and organisational innovations in packaging and distribution of goods. German legislation requiring manufacturers to take back durable goods at the end of their life has contributed to a move towards asset recovery, remanufacturing, and design for recycling.

Once governments have established the principle of environmental liability, costs may be internalised through market mechanisms with no further need for government intervention. Meanwhile, financial organisations are beginning to see environmental liability as a risk factor when considering their investments.

3.5.4. Regulations, standards and voluntary eco-efficiency improvements

The traditional approach to "end-of-pipe" pollution control is often criticised because it provides no incentive for innovation. The effect of a regulation on technical change depends heavily on the way it is designed. Andrews and Govil (1995) criticise the way particulate, SO_x and NO_x emissions from electric utilities have been regulated in succession. Utility companies resorted to control technology as the most cost-effective way to respond to each new regulation. If all of the emissions had been regulated simultaneously, or if the companies had been warned that additional controls would be introduced, it would have been more cost-effective for them to switch to cleaner generation technology.

More foresight has been used in the regulation of vehicle emissions in the United States, with the State of California taking the lead. Vehicle manufacturers are warned of future emission standards ten years or more ahead, giving them time to develop technology that meets the standards. This "technology-driving" approach to regulation has been criticised because of its potential costs to manufacturers and their customers. Nevertheless, it has been highly successful in encouraging manufacturers to develop gasoline engine technology to meet "low-emission-vehicle" and "ultra-low-emission-vehicle" standards, although the Californian Air Resources Board originally designed these standards with the intention of encouraging alternative fuel use. So far, the more restrictive requirement for manufacturers to introduce "zero emission vehicles" – *i.e.* electric vehicles – has not succeeded in making this technology a commercial competitor for gasoline vehicles.

Regulations can be designed to provide an incentive for innovation, for instance by allowing firms to trade emission permits. Examples include SO_2 allowance trading in the United States and provisions in the Montreal Protocol for "industrial rationalisation" in the production of ozone-depleting substances. The basis for trading also exists under the UN ECE Convention on Long Range Transboundary Air Pollution. The OECD has studied these programmes, seeking lessons that might be relevant for a greenhouse gas trading system (Mullins, 1997). Perhaps the best documented of these is the US sulphur trading scheme, which has helped to halve the cost of sulphur control technology.

Regulations and voluntary agreements to increase resource efficiency can have unwanted effects. A 10% energy efficiency improvement in cars would reduce the cost of driving and would stimulate about 1-4% increase in traffic (OECD, 1997*h*). The motorists' consumer surplus would increase, and energy use would be reduced, but other environmental impacts could increase. The lower costs of more eco-efficient products and services can also lead to feedback effects elsewhere in the economy. If consumers spend less on these products and services, they are likely to spend more on other goods and services, again leading to a net economic stimulus. Again, this might sometimes lead to a net increase in environmental impact. Hence, efficiency standards should be seen as *complements* rather than *alternatives* to eco-taxes.

These two instruments have different economic rationales and can be applied together. Efficiency standards (and other related measures) may be justified for refrigerators, cars and other consumer equipment as a means of overcoming transaction costs, lack of information or imperfect competition in the market (IEA, 1997*b*; OECD, 1997*h*). Eco-taxes and fiscal incentives are justified by the need to internalise environmental costs. Where the measures are combined, they are likely to achieve a net environmental improvement.

3.5.5. Physical infrastructure

The physical infrastructure can include transport and communication networks, energy supply systems and buildings. During the 20th century, governments have played a prominent role in infrastructure planning, investment and regulation. Infra-structure has a key role to play in the transition to sustainable development, as its design can influence and even constrain production and consumption patterns for decades or centuries.

The recent trend in most OECD countries towards less dense, suburban settlements, along with a strong emphasis on road provision by governments, has helped to lock people into using cars as their main means of transport. While many experts doubt that the trends will be reversed in the next century, an increasing number of communities are seeking alternative ways of meeting their mobility and access needs, for example through a shift to non-motorised or public transport (OECD, 1997*i*). These communities' chances of success are greatest where their infrastructure is easily adapted to alternative transport patterns, and allows individuals to choose more sustainable lifestyles.

Energy supply systems also have a key influence on the life-cycle impacts of consumption patterns. Historical government planning and investment decisions have locked many countries into particular energy supply options, and out of other options (OECD, 1997*b*). Governments are most likely to enable the needs of future generations to be met by ensuring that new infrastructure is designed for flexibility in energy supply.

3.5.6. Information and education

For citizens to change their behaviour as producers and consumers, they need to have some motivation, an opportunity to change, and the ability to take that opportunity (Jager *et al.*, 1997). All three of these factors depend on the extent to which citizens are educated and informed:

- motivation to improve eco-efficiency may come from knowledge of the dangers and costs of eco-inefficient production and consumption, and from shared social and cultural goals of sustainability;

- opportunities to improve eco-efficiency are no use unless individuals are aware of them: meanwhile, education that encourages creativity and initiative may enable citizens to identify new opportunities;

- the ability to take opportunities may depend on individuals' degree of technical and social competence, self-awareness, and understanding of the implications of the options available.

Information and education is a factor in the behaviour of both consumers and producers, including the many professionals who influence production patterns. Several participants in the OECD's Eco-Efficiency Workshop suggested that environmental education should be a priority. A first step might be to focus on training for professions that have large and lasting influences on infrastructure development, institutions and lifestyles. An environmental component could be included in degrees in architecture, business administration, economics, education, engineering and public administration.

Efforts are also needed to improve environmental education in schools. Dunlop (1993) emphasises the need for environmental education to be multidisciplinary, forming part of the school curriculum for both the natural and social sciences. He explains that children need to learn not only about the science of environmental problems: they also need to learn to participate effectively in the social processes that may be able to solve those problems.

Information flows are essential to the diffusion of new technology, practices and behaviour patterns. Countries vary in the quality of information available on the challenge of sustainable development and the possible action that can be taken by individuals and firms. Case studies or examples of good practice are particularly important as a means of making the information concrete and relevant. Several governments are beginning to use the Internet as a means to make information widely available and to provide a forum where local governments, firms and individuals can share their experiences.

3.5.7. Monitoring and assessing progress

A national database of environmental statistics is the first step towards understanding the size of the problem, and to finding out whether it is improving or worsening. Governments can also play a role in requiring or encouraging companies to monitor and report on their energy and materials use and pollutant releases.

It is often difficult or impossible to establish how effective a policy has been:

- responses to any policy changes, including price changes, are hard to distinguish from the effects of other influences;

- the effects of information provision, technology standards, voluntary agreements and targets are hard to distinguish from "business-as-usual", or what would have happened anyway;

- subsidies and other price incentives to adopt new technology or practices may be taken up by a large proportion of "free riders" – those who would have adopted the new technology anyway.

Evaluation tends to rely on the skilful use of detailed indicators such as energy intensity, factor prices, and investment levels, along with market surveys to evaluate the extent to which policies and measures have played a role in bringing about changes. Even with these techniques, experts may argue intensely over the true effects of a policy. The corporate average fuel economy (CAFE) standard in the United States is an obvious example.

Following the legislation for CAFE standards in 1975, and their introduction from 1978, the average fuel economy achieved by US-manufactured cars increased by about 46% to 1994. However, some analysts argue that much of this improvement was brought about by factors other than standards, including the high oil prices between 1974 and 1985, and competition from Japanese manufacturers who were selling much lower-consuming cars. The standards were important in establishing a common expectation of the direction of car technology development, but they were not the sole cause of that development.

A better understanding of the effects of measures will depend on better information-gathering, not only in the form of economic, social, environmental and other statistics, but also careful studies and surveys to evaluate particular cases. While such studies and surveys are expensive and time-consuming, they are increasingly needed. Commitments under the Kyoto Protocol may increase the need for robust evaluation of the effects of individual measures both at the project level and at the national level. The OECD often works with Member countries to analyse case studies on the effects of policies, and to develop common methodologies for evaluation. More work of this type is needed to understand the effects of policies on technical and social innovation, and the potential for improving eco-efficiency.

3.6. ECONOMIC EFFECTS OF POLICIES FOR INCREASING ECO-EFFICIENCY

Section 2 identified instances where innovation *at the level of individual firms* brought both financial and environmental benefits. It is not apparent how replicating such innovations economy-wide would affect the economy. There is a continuing active debate over the effects of environment policy on innovation. On the one hand, Harvard professor Michael Porter suggests that environmental policies such as eco-taxes and regulations lead to innovation that improves competitiveness and profit-ability (Porter and van der Linde, 1995). On the other, any constraint on industrial activity can reduce short-term profitability (Walley and Whitehead, 1994; Palmer *et al.*, 1995). There is evidence to support both arguments, depending on the indus-trial sector and time-frame being considered:

- firms in fast-changing industries have been able to use environmental man-agement systems to involve staff in creative problem-solving, leading to in-novative solutions that enhance profitability in the long term;

- firms in mature industries, with large and "lumpy" investments, have often met environmental controls through add-on technology which increases their costs. Some firms may introduce innovative technology that is cleaner, cheaper and produces a higher quality product, but other firms with capital tied up in old technology may be forced out of business.

While technical and structural change involves winners and losers at the level of the individual firm, productivity increases through technical change are seen by many economists as the source of economic growth (*e.g.*, Solow, 1962; Nelson *et al.*, 1967; Dosi *et al.*, 1988; Grossman and Helpman, 1993; Maddison, 1995). Provided that improving eco-efficiency results in higher total factor productivity, it is likely to stimulate the economy. However, links among resource, labour and capital produc-tivity remain poorly understood and need further study.

The effects on GDP of economy-wide eco-efficiency improvements remain uncertain. However, broader welfare indicators, such as "green GDP" including environmental externalities, are more likely to reveal positive effects from eco-efficiency improvements (Repetto *et al.*, 1996).

Environmental taxes and regulations are sometimes opposed on the grounds that exports will suffer, but the evidence for this is mixed. In industries for which production costs are the sole basis of competition, and where the only means of reducing pollution is through end-of-pipe controls, environmental laws may reduce competitiveness. However, experience with cleaner production and eco-efficiency programmes indicates that there are many opportunities to reduce environmental impacts and save money or improve product quality at the same time. In these cases, competitiveness may be enhanced (OECD, 1997*g*; Johnstone, 1997; Robins and Roberts, 1997). Japan is often cited as an example to show that high resource prices can stimulate productivity and improve international competitiveness. Developing cleaner and more efficient technology can open up export markets as, for example, Danish experience with wind energy demonstrates.

There are several reasons why growing trade might create new environmental challenges:

- transportation adds significantly to the life-cycle environmental impacts of some traded products, especially fresh fruit and vegetables;

- some of the approaches to increasing eco-efficiency discussed in Section 2, such as asset recovery and remanufacturing, are most effective where production occurs close to the final consumer;

- countries with high environmental standards increasingly consume goods from countries with lower environmental standards, thus effectively "exporting pollution".

There are possible counter-arguments to all of these points. For example, Robins and Roberts (1997) provide a response to the last point with case studies of instances where consumer preferences in OECD countries have influenced non-OECD country exporters to use cleaner production techniques. Meanwhile, globalisation creates opportunities for more efficient resource allocation and hence improved eco-efficiency. Reduced barriers to trade in electricity and gas markets could offer substantial environmental benefits (OECD, 1997*b*).

Participants in the OECD Eco-Efficiency Workshop (see Annex III) argued that more account should be taken of environmental and other concerns in the international discussion of trade issues. More evidence and evaluation is needed to understand the potential for integrating economic, trade, environmental and innovation policies. These are likely to be key issues for the future work of the OECD and its Member countries.

4. CONCLUSIONS

This study addresses a request from OECD Environment Ministers to assess the potential of strategies to improve eco-efficiency, and hence decouple pollutant release and resource use from economic activity.

4.1. THE POTENTIAL FOR IMPROVING ECO-EFFICIENCY IN FIRMS AND COMMUNITIES

WBCSD and its member companies have developed a business strategy to improve eco-efficiency, which involves:

- **developing specific indicators and criteria** or goals to improve environmental and resource productivity;

- working towards the goals through **innovation in technology, practices and ways of thinking**; and

- **monitoring the indicators** and modifying the strategy if necessary.

Similar strategies are also used, with different goals, by national and local governments, community groups and others, including groups of households.

Indicators of environmental and resource productivity are readily applied to the activities of manufacturers, service companies, local governments, and any other organisation or process that generates a product or service. Such indicators are less relevant to consumption patterns, for example, in households or the transport sector, where the "output" is difficult to define.

Government action is necessary to enable firms and communities to achieve the potential for improving eco-efficiency, and also to increase that potential. Without new government policies, business and other initiatives to improve eco-efficiency typically achieve energy, material and water savings in the region of 10-40%. Such initiatives reduce environmental pressure and save money at the same time. A range of government policies, including economic and regulatory instruments, can make larger savings profitable at the level of the firm. "Extended producer responsibility" schemes in particular can encourage firms to reduce environmental pressures throughout the life-cycle of their products and services. Governments can also support local eco-efficiency initiatives through policies to create a good "climate for innovation": supporting co-operative research, development and experimentation; stimulating new niche markets through public procurement, planning and tendering policies; promoting networks among companies, local governments, universities and other organisations; and providing information to bridge communication gaps.

4.2. THE POTENTIAL FOR IMPROVING ECO-EFFICIENCY ECONOMY-WIDE

Governments can and do make use of many elements of the WBCSD approach to help develop national strategies for sustainable development, since several of the goals correspond well to broader sustainable development goals. In particular, national governments are concerned directly with reducing aggregate environmental pressure, improving economic performance and enhancing quality of life, as well as improving eco-efficiency. National governments need indicators and criteria of different types to those used by firms. This implies maintaining a wide range of indicators of environmental, economic and other quality-of-life indicators. These indicators are a subset of those required to monitor progress towards sustainable development. It would be premature at this stage to suggest a standard set of indicators or a single composite indicator. The chosen indicators are likely to depend on national circumstances and aims.

Many environmental pressures have lightened in recent years in OECD Member countries, mainly as a result of government policies and structural changes. Others are worsening, notably those associated with CO_2 emissions, municipal waste, and water consumption. The "Factor 10 Club" argues that the intensity of material and energy use in the economy should be reduced by a factor of ten in industrialised countries over the next 30-50 years, in order to halve global CO_2 emissions while allowing for continuing economic growth. Although "Factor 10" may serve as an effective slogan to mobilise political support, it should not be taken literally, as energy and material use are only loosely related to specific environmental problems other than CO_2 emissions. Government efforts are needed to establish sustainable development goals and indicators linked to specific concerns.

Rapid gains in labour, energy and material productivity have occasionally occurred across whole sectors or economies in OECD Member countries. These gains can be in the range 4-8% per year, which would lead to four- to ten-fold improvements if they were maintained over 30 years. Over the longer term, OECD economies have achieved average labour productivity increases of 2-3% per year over 200 years, increasing incomes ten-fold while halving working hours. The report finds that high rates of innovation are stimulated by strong competitive pressures; high factor prices or regulatory incentives; a process of catching up with "best practice"; and the presence of a good "climate for innovation". However, achieving such a coherent set of stimuli for improvements in eco-efficiency would require a very strong political and popular will.

Where ministries give conflicting signals to market actors, they are unlikely to prompt coherent action to improve eco-efficiency. Many policies provide the wrong incentives, such as high taxes on employment and protection against competition for resource-intensive industries. Achieving rapid eco-efficiency improvements is likely to depend on governments establishing goals that are shared by all ministries and other public agencies. The OECD has consistently recommended that governments reform subsidies, taxes and regulation to bring prices into line with long-run marginal social costs. It is also important to ensure that market actors' rights and responsibilities are consistent with sustainable development goals. Member countries have found the concepts of "extended" and "shared" producer responsibility particularly useful in reducing environmental impacts linked to consumption patterns. Governments can further encourage the development of more eco-efficient technologies and practices through environmental education and training for key professionals, including engineers, architects and teachers.

Faced with a very complex set of goals, interests and inter-relationships in the economy, government strategies are most likely to succeed if they are broadly based, using a mix of instruments; inclusive, ensuring that stakeholders are involved in policy design and implementation; tolerant of experimentation and occasional failure; and adaptive, using monitoring and feedback mechanisms to adjust measures whenever necessary.

4.3. NEXT STEPS

This report has mapped out some of the issues surrounding eco-efficiency and strategies to improve it. Such strategies may well have the potential to "decouple pollutant release and resource use from economic activity", in the OECD Environment Ministers' words. The policies of OECD Member governments will have a considerable influence on the extent to which that potential is reached. In order to improve the design, coherence, and implementation of those policies, there is a need for further effort on several fronts:

- identifying and assessing approaches to developing shared goals, targets and criteria, at an international, national and local level;

- evaluating policies and programmes for encouraging changes in technology, practices and ways of thinking that can help to achieve the goals;

- examining the approaches used in businesses, governments and other organisations to monitor and evaluate policies and programmes.

Further research is also required to understand the potential for improving eco-efficiency on both a sectoral and an economy-wide basis, and the implications for the economy and for sustainable development.

One way forward would be for the OECD to embark on a process of constructing scenarios to illustrate current trends and possible routes to sustainable development. The work would need to involve representatives from different parts of Member country governments. This process would build on existing OECD efforts, such as the Linkages project (OECD, 1997g) and scenarios for environmentally sustainable transport. It could also draw on the experience from scenario-building efforts in other organisations, such as the Intergovernmental Panel on Climate Change (IPCC, 1995), the UN Environment Programme (UNEP, 1997) and WBCSD (1997).

Construction of scenarios could be a vehicle to discuss the choice of *goals, indicators and criteria for sustainable development*, the processes involved in achieving those goals, and the role of government in those processes. In considering the role of government, the scenarios would need to make use of policy analysis that has already been carried out by the OECD, but could also draw on *new case study material* from Member countries.

There is a need for a more systematic *exchange of information on national efforts* to promote eco-efficiency improvements through innovation. Such an exchange would enable governments to learn from each other's experiences and would help to identify opportunities for co-operation. This exchange of information could take place through existing programmes in the OECD. Finally, further work is needed in the Organisation and in Member countries to *develop and apply rigorous methods for monitoring and evaluating* the effects of policies and programmes.

Annex I
MEETING HUMAN NEEDS
AND BRINGING QUALITY OF LIFE?

Differing views of "human needs" contribute to controversy in environmental politics. "Basic" needs may be universal, including food, shelter, clean water, and can perhaps extend to social and political needs (*e.g.* Doyal and Gough, 1991). Such needs are enshrined in statements of "human rights", such as the 1945 United Nations Charter. Their fulfilment can be measured, for example, through the percentage of a population that has access to clean water or sewerage, or the share of household income needed for basic nutrition.

Marketing of products and services is usually designed to activate "needs" in a different sense: that of psychological motivators. There are several models of needs and motivation. Maslow (1954) described a "hierarchy" of needs: food and shelter; security; belongingness; esteem; self-actualisation. According to Maslow, when needs such as food and shelter are not met, they form stronger motivators than needs such as self-actualisation. Individuals differ in their requirements to satisfy a particular need. Other researchers have developed similar models using different classification systems and explanations (*e.g.* Allardt, 1993).

Having a good "quality of life" does not necessarily mean meeting needs. It may come from working to fulfil them. Some individuals find a good quality of life by letting go of needs through spiritual practices. Ownership of some types of good may improve quality of life (OECD, 1996a). Some writers have questioned whether material goods satisfy human needs. Fromm (1956) used murder, suicide and alcoholism statistics to suggest that the wealthiest OECD societies had the lowest quality of life. Kempton and Payne (1997) argue that material goods have become status (esteem) symbols because communities are too large to show traditional, tribal forms of esteem.

Economic analysis generally deals with concepts such as "need" and "quality of life" via utility theory. According to theory, utility or welfare cannot be measured directly, but changes in welfare associated with acquiring goods are revealed in the market prices of those goods. If markets were perfect and all goods were traded (under full competition, full information, no externalities and no transaction costs), firms would be able to measure the extent to which they are meeting human needs through their revenue. Societal welfare would be represented by GDP. However, markets are not perfect: information gaps and transaction costs abound (Jacobs, 1994; Stern, 1986); government policies result in additional rigidities and distortions (OECD, 1997b); and consumers and other market actors often perceive themselves to have no choice in the means of meeting their needs (Lutzenheiser and Shove, 1996).

Many attempts have been made to develop indicators that can complement or replace GDP. A wide range of socio-economic indicators can complement GDP, including income distribution statistics, educational success and employment rates. Possible GDP substitutes such as "green national accounts" usually take account of unpriced goods and services or externalities. For example, the accounts are augmented by the value of unpaid housework, but reduced by environmental externalities.

Annex II

PROGRESS IN POLLUTION PREVENTION

This annex briefly reviews trends in pollution in OECD countries.

AGRICULTURAL TRENDS

Productivity was the overriding agriculture policy concern during most of this century in OECD countries. Most countries have used a broad range of incentives to support farmers and have invested in R&D to develop high-yielding crops. These policies were successful, with the well-known consequence of food surpluses, especially in Europe during the 1980s and early 1990s. Productivity was achieved at some cost to the environment, with tillage leading to soil erosion, nitrogen fertilisers contributing to high nitrate levels in groundwater, and the combination of pesticides and habitat destruction leading to a loss of genetic diversity. Agricultural land use and other inputs have declined slightly in recent years as a result of agricultural policy reforms. Insecticide use has declined in many countries by 50% or more, although fungicide use has increased. Farmers are using marginally smaller amounts of nitrogen fertilisers than in the 1980s but there is no strong trend, while phosphate fertiliser use is falling, now to about 20% below the level of the mid-80s. Between 1980 and 1994, the area of agricultural land declined slightly, with more land under forest cover, but the area of irrigated land increased by 14%. Stocks of sheep and cows have fallen by about 10% (OECD, 1997f).

TOXIC RELEASE: AIR POLLUTION

Air pollutants such as particulates, carbon monoxide, VOCs and NO_x are generally following a downward trend in OECD countries. For mobile sources (cars and trucks) the reductions have resulted mainly from government regulations. In stationary sources' fuel switching from coal and oil to natural gas and electricity has played a strong role.

One recent OECD study (OECD, 1995*a*) evaluated countries' policies on the control of hazardous air pollutants. Countries for which case studies were carried out have either achieved, or expect to achieve, reductions in a variety of emissions, at rates typically of the order of a halving every decade. If this rate could be sustained, emissions would fall ten-fold in three to four decades. However, it should not be concluded that ten-fold reductions in these emissions are possible or easy to attain: in most cases, the reductions reported or projected here represent the results of the first attempts to monitor and control the emissions. Further emission reductions may be harder to achieve.

FRESHWATER ABSTRACTION

Abstractions of fresh water have been fairly stable in OECD countries since 1980. This overall trend hides local pressures on fresh water supply, which are becoming extreme in several OECD countries. Meanwhile, there has been an increase in consumption from public water supplies and a decline in water use by industry. Consumption from public supplies increased at a rate of approximately 2.3% per year during the 1980s, slightly slower than GDP, in six major OECD countries (Canada, France, Italy, Japan, Spain, United Kingdom, United States).

MATERIAL FLOWS

The World Resources Institute has collected national information on total material requirements (TMR) in Germany, Japan, the Netherlands, and the United States (WRI, 1997). In addition to direct material inputs to the economy in the form of traded commodities, TMR includes "hidden" material flows that never enter the economy.[*] "Hidden" flows include material such as the overburden removed during surface mining, the branches, leaves and roots discarded during forest clearance, and the soil erosion due to agriculture. Total flows are a factor of three to five times larger than commodity flows in the four countries.

TMR measures the mass of material used but does not involve any ecological weighting for different types of material or different types of flow. Materials that are merely disturbed are counted alongside those that are physically and chemically processed. This highlights a major difficulty in measuring material intensity: some material flows have more ecological impact than others. Researchers have so far made little progress in establishing the link between TMR and environmental damage.

---

66   *   These flows are not at all hidden from those close to them.

A more interesting indicator from the perspective of environmental impacts is the level of material *movement*. In Germany and the United States, domestic freight transport has kept pace with GDP over the last 30 years, although in Japan the increase has been slightly slower than that of GDP.

Long-distance international freight transport, mainly by sea, is growing about twice as fast as domestic freight. This indicator is of particular interest as a symptom of globalisation, and of the increasing spatial separation between production and consumption. Crude oil traffic has not yet recovered its pre-oil shock levels, but dry bulk traffic (mostly ores and grain) and "other" traffic have increased at around 4% per year in the last decade. Although the "other" category is small in volume, it accounts for the majority of trade in value, including manufactured goods and food other than bulk grain.

A very large share of world shipments are from or to an OECD country. Only 16% of the total volume is between two non-OECD countries. Over half of these raw material shipments are from Australia and North America, although an increasing share are coming from non-OECD countries.

World air freight traffic (tonne-km on scheduled services) has grown particularly rapidly, at 11.7% per year from 1960 to reach 95 billion tonne-km in 1990 (ICAO, 1995). Although this figure is a factor of 200 smaller than total maritime traffic, air freight globally uses about half as much energy as maritime freight. OECD country-registered airlines account for about four-fifths of world air traffic.

WASTE AND RECYCLING

The generation of municipal and hazardous waste is growing more quickly than the use of materials in the OECD, although the picture varies among Member countries. Municipal waste generation increased by 40% between 1980 and 1995, although the increase was very slight in some countries such as Japan.

Conversely, a growing amount of material is recycled: the proportions of paper and glass recycled now exceed 50% of consumption in some countries (OECD, 1997f).

ENERGY INTENSITY TRENDS

Indicators of energy use are better developed and less controversial than most. Energy use per capita has been almost constant in OECD countries over the last 25 years. Industrial energy use has declined but transport sector energy use has increased. While industrial and residential/commercial energy use do not appear to be coupled to GDP, transport energy use per unit of GDP has been stationary for most of the period, although it fell slightly during the period of high oil prices (1974-1985).

Annex III
OECD WORKSHOP ON ECO-EFFICIENCY: MAIN FINDINGS

USEFULNESS OF THE CONCEPT OF ECO-EFFICIENCY

Definition

Eco-efficiency is open to a variety of interpretations. Some companies and governments use the term so that it is virtually synonymous with "cleaner production". The focus on the *function* of products and services for the consumer is similar to that in "life-cycle management". Other companies have used eco-efficiency in a way that brings new meaning, in particular by emphasising the dynamic of *innovation* in technology and organisation. Some workshop participants suggested that the OECD should define eco-efficiency more tightly, perhaps as an indicator such as value added per unit of environmental impact. Others felt that the breadth of meaning was an advantage, allowing many stakeholders with differing interests to sign up to strategies for eco-efficiency.

The OECD background report noted that eco-efficiency aims to meet the needs of *businesses, consumers* and the *environment*. It was emphasised in the workshop that strategies for eco-efficiency will fail if they neglect any one of these three interests. Some participants questioned the extent to which consumers have so far been involved in discussions about their needs. Businesses often invent new needs for consumers by developing and marketing new products and services. Consumers are rarely involved in consideration of the trade-off between developing new needs and moving towards environmental sustainability.

Eco-efficiency is necessary, but not sufficient, for sustainable development. The Brundtland Commission also emphasised the need to improve equity, reduce poverty, encourage democracy and support human rights. Whereas WBCSD aims to use eco-efficiency improvements to reduce resource use and environmental damage to levels within the earth's carrying capacity, the Brundtland Commission also emphasised the need to *build up* stocks of natural capital.

Indicators

One of the key attractions of eco-efficiency is the emphasis placed on indicators, bearing in mind the maxim that "what's measured gets managed". Indicators can take a multitude of forms depending on their function and audience. Firms need different indicators from those used by governments, reflecting their different scales and types of concern. Efficiency and intensity indicators are important for comparing products, services, firms and sectors. Such indicators are likely to be particularly useful for firms reviewing their own performance and competitiveness. Substance flow and state-of-the-environment indicators are more useful for measuring national and international progress towards sustainable development.

Simple, qualitative indicators may be useful for decision-making purposes, especially when searching for products and services that offer large improvements in eco-efficiency. Detailed, quantitative indicators are likely to be needed by governments to monitor environmental quality and identify emerging challenges.

Although governments and intergovernmental organisations will need to use indicators, many participants felt that it would be premature at this stage to standardise indicators, suggesting that it would be more appropriate to develop measurement and reporting systems that can evolve over time. Companies and governments can learn about the environmental and management problems they are considering by developing their own indicators. Meanwhile, participants cautioned against the choice of oversimplified indicators or developing a single indicator of eco-efficiency. They pointed to the example of GDP as an indicator which governments sometimes try to maximise to the detriment of other important objectives.

Some of the dimensions of eco-efficiency identified by WBCSD were thought to be inappropriate for general advocacy. Moving from products to services and extending product durability will not always reduce resource use and environmental impacts. The emphasis should be on reducing the material, energy and pollution intensity of products and services on a life-cycle basis. Indicators of service delivered and welfare remain controversial, although approaches such as social cost accounting should continue to be pursued.

THE POTENTIAL OF ECO-EFFICIENCY TO DECOUPLE ECONOMIC ACTIVITY FROM RESOURCE USE AND ENVIRONMENTAL DAMAGE

Targets: Factor 4/Factor 10

Advocates of Factor 4 and Factor 10 improvements in eco-efficiency base their arguments on the aim of halving total resource use by about 2025-2040. They justify this aim mainly with reference to greenhouse gas emissions. A halving of CO_2 emissions by 2040 would be consistent with a longer term aim of stabilising atmospheric CO_2 concentrations at 350-450 ppm. Workshop participants did not feel that it was justified to extend the aim as a specific, quantitative target for other forms of environmental damage and resource use, although they recognised its value for signalling the need for fundamental change.

Advocacy of Factor 10 resource efficiency improvements in OECD countries is based on equity arguments. OECD countries now contain about a fifth of the world population, and by 2050 this fraction may shrink towards a tenth.[*] Yet these countries consume about a half of the world's energy supply and emit half the CO_2 emissions. Thus, if emissions were to be halved and emissions per capita were to be evenly spread, OECD citizens would have to reduce their emissions by a factor of 10. Again, it is not clear that this argument extends to other resources or environmental impacts.

A Factor 4 target has the advantage of appearing achievable. It is relatively easy to identify technical and organisational changes that can achieve 75% reductions in resource use or environmental impact, but harder to find changes that can achieve 90% reductions. It can also be considered separately from the equity argument.

Dynamics of improving eco-efficiency

Innovation in technology, organisation and institutions is the key dynamic in improving eco-efficiency. The innovation process includes not only the development of new technologies, but their successful deployment and diffusion. While some workshop participants expressed the view that "breakthrough" innovation would be needed to achieve targets such as Factor 10, others emphasised that *all* types of innovation in technology, behaviour and organisation will be needed.

---

[*] In fact, UN population projections have recently been revised downwards, suggesting figures in the region of 7.7-10 billion in 2040, of which 10-15% might be in industrialised countries.

Apparent obstacles to improving eco-efficiency include the first cost of new technologies; the current system of alliances among stakeholders that tends to preserve the status quo; the presence of market and intervention failures and inefficiencies; and inefficient communication within and among firms.

The phenomenon of technological, behavioural and institutional "lock-in" makes any change look costly, although large changes may be possible with no cost, or even savings. The challenge is to tunnel through the cost barrier or to avoid it by taking advantage of changes that are occurring anyway. Rapid changes are occurring in society, with the rapid take-off of communication and information technology, the emergence of biotechnology and other scientific/commercial breakthroughs. Markets and styles of management and organisation are also changing, while consumer groups are strengthening and beginning consciously to define their own "needs". Collectively, these trends have been described as a move towards a "knowledge-based" economy. While these changes will not necessarily lead to a more eco-efficient society, they offer an opportunity to move in that direction.

It was suggested that some large companies, especially market leaders, prefer to change their products gradually and that more adventurous innovations may come from companies ranked third or fourth in market share. An economy-wide move towards improved eco-efficiency would probably mean that some products and firms disappeared and new ones emerged. The fear of being among the losers can lead to a business culture that discourages change. There is a perception that "the environment doesn't sell", although some participants suggested that few firms have tried wholeheartedly to sell it. Participants also mentioned that the governments of some commodity-exporting countries have expressed concern in United Nations forums that their exports would be reduced by a move towards improved eco-efficiency.

Several participants mentioned the innovation-stifling effects of government subsidies and other policies supporting polluting activities, referring to recent studies by the Earth Council and the OECD. Subsidy reform, green tax reform, and the creation of futures markets in environmental goods were discussed as important parts of the dynamic for eco-efficiency improvement.

Most of the well-known companies with eco-efficiency programmes are large multinationals with strong internal systems for innovation. Communication gaps among accounting units or businesses can act as barriers to the innovation process. This applies especially to the failure to educate sales staff about the environmental performance of products – a key step if those staff are to market more eco-efficient products. Small and medium-sized enterprises (SMEs) tend to be handicapped by limited access to information. Smaller companies may also have less access to capital than large ones, making it harder to develop and market new products.

THE ROLE OF GOVERNMENT IN STRATEGIES FOR ECO-EFFICIENCY

The role of government is changing along with the other shifts currently under way in society. Many governments may seem to have less power *vis-à-vis* the growing transnational companies. However, governments can learn from the management philosophies of these companies. In addition to the government's traditional concern with markets and to establish rights and liabilities, its contribution to education, communication, networking and facilitation are essential. A key responsibility of government is to ensure that priorities in the national system for innovation reflect the need for improved eco-efficiency.

Many participants emphasised the part played by governments in posing obstacles to eco-efficiency, through subsidies and other interventions that encourage resource use and pollution. Participants also discussed the need for governments to develop coherent policies, rallying all ministries around the principle of sustainable development. One suggestion made in the workshop was that governments could create independent institutions for sustainable development. Such institutions might have a monitoring and auditing role for government, businesses and other organisations.

Governments may also have a special role to play in relation to small and medium-sized enterprises and in the service sector. These groups of businesses have traditionally been subject to less environmental pressure than large companies, and probably offer the greatest opportunities for eco-efficiency improvement. Those governments that have targeted SMEs have found that "eco-efficiency" is an easily understood and well-received concept. Their eco-efficiency programmes have been successful in achieving large reductions in waste and pollution, while reducing costs and stimulating innovation.

Some participants identified a need to shift the focus of government policies from the supply side to the demand side, for example through education and by developing better links with stakeholder groups. Education is also important for workers and others; environmental courses could be included in business, engineering, and public administration degrees.

Initiatives may increasingly occur at the local level. More effort is needed to develop a climate for technical and social innovation by providing strong signals about the need for action and by encouraging the flow of information and ideas. New media such as the Internet are making it easier for governments to play this type of role.

THE OECD'S ROLE

The OECD has a multiple role to play:

- Improving governments' understanding of the potential role of eco-efficiency in relation to sustainable development and raising its profile, partly by developing a coherent position in-house that is shared by all Committees and Directorates.

- Analysing the effectiveness of policies in improving eco-efficiency. Additional attention is needed for strategies and systems for innovation, information, education, and research. There is considerable potential for co-operation among existing OECD Committees working on environment, industrial innovation policy, education and consumer affairs. Subsidy and tax reform will be a crucial component, but more work is needed on the role of different stakeholders, including SMEs and environmental and consumer NGOs. Analysis is also needed of the trade, equity, and other economic impacts of eco-efficiency.

- Collecting and publicising data and working with stakeholder groups to develop useful indicators of eco-efficiency.

- Acting as a mediator among Member countries and a bridge to the broader intergovernmental community and to other stakeholder groups, including consumer organisations and trade unions.

Annex IV

EXAMPLES OF ECO-EFFICIENCY MENTIONED IN THIS REPORT

COMPANY AND OTHER NGO INITIATIVES

Bayer: waste-free production of synthetic rubber

British Telecom: no-refrigerant cooling; paper saving

Dow: Waste Reduction Always Pays programme (WRAP); Eco-compass; Rent-a-Chemical

Electricité de France: selling electricity end-use services instead of electricity

GAP: the Eco-Team approach

Glaxo Wellcome: Waste Elimination Teams

Greenpeace: the GreenFreeze refrigerator; the SMILe car

IBM: asset recovery

ING: environmental management system

Interface Flooring Systems: replaceable carpet squares

3M: Pollution Prevention Pays programme (3P)

MIT: Re-usable paper and ink

Mitsubishi: gasoline direct injection engine

Northern Telecom:	Lead-free soldering
Philips:	Green television
Roche:	Eco-Efficiency Ratio
Siemens-Nixdorf:	asset recovery
Sony:	remanufacturing
Xerox:	asset recovery/remanufacturing

GOVERNMENT INITIATIVES

Australia:	Cleaner Production Programme; handbook on cleaner production for local government; Green Health Guide
Canada:	National Round Table for the Environment and the Economy: government-industry consultation on indicators
Denmark:	tax on non-hazardous waste
Germany:	take-back legislation for manufacturers
Netherlands:	packaging ordnance; four ministries' joint policy document on sustainable development
New Zealand:	tradable fishing allowances
Norway:	CO_2 tax; GRIP centre for sustainable production and consumption; eco-profiles for buildings
Portugal:	work on eco-efficiency with SMEs
Sweden:	stakeholder approach to define and target "environmentally sustainable transport"; sulphur tax
United Kingdom:	subsidy and regulatory reform; cleaner production best practice programme; Non-Fossil Fuel Obligation

United States: Green Chemistry Challenge; Intermodal Surface Transportation Efficiency Act; Partnership for a New Generation of Vehicles; Energy Star; SO_2 emission permit trading scheme

REFERENCES

Allardt, E. (1993), "Having, loving, being: an alternative to the Swedish model of welfare research", in Nussbaum and Sen (1993).

Andrews, C.J. and S. Govil (1995), "Becoming proactive about environmental risks: Regulatory reform and risk management in the US electricity sector", Energy Policy Vol. 23, No. 10, pp. 885-892.

Baron, R..(1997), Economic/Fiscal Instruments: Competitiveness Issues Related to Carbon/ Energy Taxation, Policies and Measures for Possible Common Action, Working Paper 14, IEA/OECD, Paris.

BCSD [Business Council for Sustainable Development] (1993), Getting Eco-Efficient, Report of the Business Council for Sustainable Development, First Antwerp Eco-Efficiency Workshop, November 1993, BCSD, Geneva.

Burniaux, J.-M., J. Martin, and J. Oliveira-Martins (1992), "The effects of existing distortions in energy markets on the cost of policies to reduce CO_2 emissions: evidence from GREEN", OECD Economic Studies, Winter, pp. 141-165.

Costanza, R., R. d'Arge, R. de Groot, S. Farber, M. Grasso, B. Hannon, K. Limburg, S. Naeem, R. V. O'Neill, J. Paruelo, R. G. Raskin, P. Sutton and M. van den Belt (1997), "The value of the world's ecoystem services and natural capital", Nature, Vol. 387, No. 6630, p. 253.

DeLuchi, M.A. (1992), Hydrogen Fuel-Cell Vehicle,. Research Report UCD-ITS-RR-92-14, Institute of Transportation Studies, University of California at Davis, Davis, CA.

de Moor, A. and P. Calamai (1996), Subsidising Unsustainable Development: Undermining the Earth with Public Funds, Institute for Research on Public Expenditure, The Hague and Earth Council, San José, Costa Rica.

DeSimone, L.D. and F. Popoff with WBCSD (1997), Eco-Efficiency: The Business Link to Sustainable Development, MIT Press, Cambridge, MA, and London.

Dosi, G., C. Freeman, R. Nelson, G. Silverberg and L. Soete (eds.) (1988), *Technical Change and Economic Theory*, Pinter, London and New York.

Doyal, L. and I. Gough (1991), A *Theory of Human Need*, ICS, London.

Dunlop, J. (1993), "Lessons from environmental education in industrialised countries", in *Environmental Education: An Approach to Sustainable Development*, OECD, Paris.

DuPont (1997), "Safety, health and the environment: part of our business", *Dupont Magazine* No. 2, *Special Issue: Dupont in Europe, Year in Review*, 1996, DuPont, Geneva.

Environment Australia (1996), *Getting Ahead of the Game: An Anticipatory Approach to Environmental Management*, A Cleaner Production Handbook for Local Government, Environment Australia, Canberra.

ERM [Environmental Resources Management] (1996), *Eco-efficiency in the Transport Sector: Applying the Concept to Public Policy and Individual Travel*, Contractor's report to the OECD, ERM, Oxford, England.

Fish, K. (1997), Presentation to OECD Workshop on "Fostering Eco-Efficiency: the Role of Government", Paris, 3-4 September (see Annex III).

Freeman, C. (1987), *Technology Policy and Economic Performance: Lessons from Japan*, Pinter, London and New York.

Freeman, C. and C. Perez (1988), "Structural crises of adjustment: business cycles and investment behaviour", in. Dosi *et al.* (1998).

Fromm, E. (1956), *The Sane Society* (second edition 1991), Routlege, London.

Fussler, C. (1996), *Driving Eco-Innovation*, Pitman Publishing, London.

Greenpeace (1997), *Energy Subsidies in Europe: How Governments Use Taxpayers' Money to Promote Climate Change and Nuclear Risk*, Greenpeace International Climate Campaign, Amsterdam.

Grossman, G. M. and E. Helpman (1993), *Endogenous Innovation in the Theory of Growth*, National Bureau of Economic Research (NBER), Working Paper No. 4527, NBER, Cambridge, MA.

ICAO [International Civil Aviation Organisation] (1995), *Outlook for Air Transport to the Year* 2003, Circular 252-AT/103, ICAO, Montreal.

ICLEI [International Council for Local Environmental Initiatives] (1997), *Local Government Implementation of Climate Protection: Report to the United Nations*, ICLEI, Toronto.

IEA [International Energy Agency] (1997a), *Indicators of Energy Use and Efficiency*, OECD, Paris.

IEA (1997b), *Enhancing the Market Deployment of Energy Technology: A Survey of Eight Technologies*, OECD, Paris.

IPCC [Intergovernmental Panel on Climate Change] (1995), *Climate Change 1994*, Cambridge University Press, Cambridge, UK.

IPCC [Intergovernmental Panel on Climate Change] (1996), *Technologies, Policies and Measures for Mitigating Climate Change*, R. T. Watson, M. C. Zinyowera and R. H. Moss (eds.), IPCC, Geneva.

IPCC (1997), *Stabilisation of Atmospheric Greenhouse Gases: Physical, Biological and Socio-Economic Implications*, IPCC Technical Paper III, J. T. Houghton, L. G. Meira Filho, D.J. Griggs and K. Maskell (eds.), IPCC, Geneva.

Jacobs, M. (1994), "The limits to neoclassicism: towards an institutional environmental economics", in M. Redclift and T. Benton (eds.), *Social Theory and the Global Environment*, Routledge, London.

Jaeger, C. (1997), Presentation to OECD Workshop on "Fostering Eco-Efficiency: the Role of Government", Paris, 3-4 September (see Annex III).

Jager, W., M.B.A. van Asselt, J. Rotmans, C.A.J. Vlek and P. Costerman Boodt (1997), *Consumer Behaviour: A Modelling Perspective in the Context of Integrated Assessment of Global Change*, Global Dynamics and Sustainable Development Programme, Globo Report Series No. 17, RIVM Report No. 461502017, RIVM, Bilthoven, Netherlands.

Johnstone, N. (1997) "Globalisation, technology and environment", Presentation to the OECD Workshop on Economic Globalisation and Environment, Vienna, 30-31 January.

Kempton, W. and C. Payne (1997), "Cultural and social evolutionary determinants of consumption", in P. Stern, T. Dietz, V. Ruttan, R. Socolow and J. Sweeney (eds.), *Environmentally Significant Consumption*, National Academy Press, Washington, DC, pp. 116-123.

Kienitz, R. (1997), "Applying eco-efficiency to personal travel behaviour: three US experiments", Presentation to the OECD Workshop on "Eco-Efficiency in Transport", Berlin, 6-7 July.

Kroon, P. (1997), Presentation to OECD Workshop on "Fostering Eco-Efficiency: the Role of Government", Paris, 3-4 September (see Annex III).

Larsen, B. and A. Shah (1992), *World Fossil Fuel Subsidies and Global Carbon Emissions*, Policy Research Working Paper Series No. 1002, World Bank, Washington.

Lovins, A.B., J.W. Barnett and L.H. Lovins (1993), *Supercars, the Coming Light-Vehicle Revolution*, Rocky Mountain Institute, Snowmass, CO.

Lundvall, B.Å. (1988), "Innovation as an interactive process: from user-producer interaction to the national system of innovation", in Dosi *et al.*, 1988, Chapter 17.

Lutzenheiser, L. and E. Shove (1996), "Individual travel behaviour: the very idea", Presentation at OECD Workshop on "Individual Travel Behaviour: Culture, Choice and Technology", Brighton, July.

MacKenzie, J.J. (1994), *The Keys to the Car*, World Resources Institute, Washington, DC.

Maddison, A. (1995), *Monitoring the World Economy 1820-1992*, Development Centre Studies, OECD, Paris.

Maslow, A. (1954), *Motivation and Personality*, Harper and Row, New York.

Merck Family Fund (1995), *Yearning for Balance: Views of Americans on Consumption, Materialism and the Environment*, Merck Family Fund, Takoma Park, MD.

Milani, B. (1997), Presentation to OECD Workshop on "Fostering Eco-Efficiency: the Role of Government", Paris, 3-4 September (see Annex III).

Ministère de l'Environnement (1997), *Guide "Maîtriser les consommations et les dépenses d'eau dans le patrimoine immobilier de l'État"*, Ministère de l'Environnement, Paris.

Mullins, F.L. (1997), *Lessons from existing trading systems for international GHG emission trading*, Information Paper for the Annex I Expert Group on the UN FCCC, OECD, Paris.

Nelson, R.R. (ed.) (1982), *Government and Technical Progress*, Pergamon, New York.

Nelson, R.R., M. J. Peck and E. D. Kalachek (1967), *Technology, Economic Growth and Public Policy*, The Brookings Institute, Washington, DC.

NRTEE [Canada's National Round Table on the Environment and the Economy] (1997), *Measuring Eco-efficiency in Business: Developing a Core Set of Eco-efficiency*

Indicators, Report on the Proceedings of the Eco-efficiency Measurement Workshop, 2 April 1997, Washington, DC, NRTEE, Ottawa.

Nussbaum, M. and Sen, A.K. (eds.) (1993), *The Quality of Life*, Clarendon Press, Oxford.

OECD [Organisation for Economic Co-operation and Development] (1972), *Recommendation of the Council on Guiding Principles Concerning International Economic Aspects of Environmental Policies*, Document C(72)128, OECD, Paris.

OECD (1974), *Recommendation of the Council on the Implementation of the Polluter-Pays Principle*, Document C(74)223, OECD, Paris.

OECD (1975), *The Polluter Pays Principle: Definition; Analysis; Implementation*, OECD, Paris.

OECD (1993), *Taxation and the Environment: Complementary Policies*, OECD, Paris.

OECD (1995a), *Control of Hazardous Air Pollutants in OECD Countries*, OECD, Paris.

OECD (1995b), *Best Practices Guide for Cleaner Production Programmes in Central and Eastern Europe*, OCDE/GD(95)98, OECD, Paris.

OECD (1996a), *OECD Economies at a Glance: Structural Indicators*, OECD, Paris.

OECD (1996b), *Pollutant Release and Transfer Registers. Guidance Manual for Governments*, OCDE/GD(96)32, OECD, Paris.

OECD (1996c), *First OECD Workshop on Individual Travel Behaviour: "Values, Welfare and Quality of Life"*, Final Report, OCDE/GD(96)199, OECD, Paris.

OECD (1997a), *Sustainable Consumption and Production: Clarifying the Concepts*, Report of a Workshop in Rosendal, Norway, 2-4 July 1995, OECD, Paris.

OECD (1997b), *Reforming Energy and Transport Subsidies*, OECD, Paris.

OECD (1997c), *Environmental Taxes and Green Tax Reform*, OECD, Paris.

OECD (1997d), *Evaluating Economic Instruments for Environmental Policy*, OECD, Paris.

OECD (1997e), *Sustainable Consumption and Individual Travel Behaviour*, Report of an OECD Policy Meeting, Paris, 9-10 January, 1997, OCDE/GD(97)144, OECD, Paris.

OECD (1997f), *OECD Environmental Data: Compendium*, 1997, OECD, Paris.

83

OECD (1997g), *The World in 2020: Towards a New Global Age*, OECD, Paris.

OECD (1997h), CO_2 *Emissions from Road Vehicles*, OCDE/GD(97)69, OECD, Paris.

OECD (1997i), *Policies and Measures to Encourage Innovation in Transport Behaviour and Technology*, OCDE/GD(97)79, OECD, Paris.

OECD (1997j), *Special Issues in Carbon/Energy Taxation: Carbon Charges on Aviation Fuels*, OCDE/GD(97)78, OECD, Paris.

Palmer, K., W.E. Oats and P.R. Portney (1995), "Tightening environmental standards: the benefit-cost or the no-cost paradigm?", *Journal of Economic Perspectives*, Vol. 9, No. 4, pp. 119-132.

Peneda, M. (1997), Presentation to OECD Workshop on "Fostering Eco-Efficiency: the Role of Government", Paris, 3-4 September (see Annex III).

Porter, M. E. and C. van der Linde (1995), "Toward a new conception of the environment-competitiveness relationship", *Journal of Economic Perspectives*, Vol. 9, No. 4. pp. 97-118.

Repetto, R., D. Rothman, P. Faeth and D. Austin (1996), *Has Environmental Protection Really Reduced Productivity Growth?* World Resources Institute, Washington, DC.

Robins, N. and S. Roberts (eds.) (1997), *Unlocking Trade Opportunities: Case Studies of Export Success from Developing Countries*, International Institute for Environment and Development, London and UN Department of Policy Co-ordination and Sustainable Development, New York.

Roodman, D. (1996), *Paying the Piper: Subsidies, Politics, and the Environment*, Worldwatch Paper 133, The Worldwatch Institute, Washington, DC.

Rosenberg, N. (1991), "Critical issues in science policy research", *Science and Public Policy*, Vol. 18, No. 6, pp. 335-346.

Rosenberg, N. (1994), *Exploring the Black Box*, Cambridge University Press, Cambridge.

Schmidheiny, S. (1992), *Changing Course*, MIT Press, Cambridge, MA.

Schumpeter, J.A. (1943), *Capitalism, Socialism, and Democracy*, George Allen and Unwin, London.

SEPA [Swedish Environmental Protection Agency] (1996), *Towards an Environmentally Sustainable Transport System*, Report 4682, Swedish Environmental Protection Agency, Stockholm.

Smith, A.C., G.P. Marsh and E.B. Beckman (1997), *Common Actions for Renewable Electricity Generation*, Draft Report by the Energy Technology Support Unit, Harwell, UK, prepared under contract for the IEA, Paris.

Smith, H. (1997), Presentation to OECD Workshop on "Fostering Eco-Efficiency: the Role of Government", Paris, 3-4 September (see Annex III).

Staats, H. J. and P. Harland (1995), *The Ecoteam Program in the Netherlands. Study 4: A Longitudinal Study on the Effects of the EcoTeam Program on Environmental Behaviour and its Psychological Backgrounds*, Summary Report, E&M/R-95/57, Centre for Energy and Environmental Research, Faculty of Social and Behavioural Sciences, Leiden University, the Netherlands.

Stern, P.C. (1986), "Blind spots in policy analysis: what economics doesn't say about energy use", *Journal of Policy Analysis and Management*, Vol. 5, No. 2, pp. 200-227.

Solow, R.M. (1962), "Technical progress, capital formation, and economic growth", *American Economic Review*, Vol. 52, No 2.

Tuppen, C. (1997), Presentation to OECD Workshop on "Fostering Eco-Efficiency: the Role of Government", Paris, 3-4 September (see Annex III).

UNCED [United Nations Conference on Environment and Development] (1992), *The Rio Declaration*, United Nations, New York.

UNDP [United Nations Development Programme] (1997), *Human Development Report*, Oxford University Press, New York and Oxford, England.

UNEP [United Nations Environment Programme] (1994), *Country and Environmental Reporting*, Technical Report No. 24, UNEP Industry and Environment, Paris.

UNEP (1997), *Global Environmental Outlook*, Oxford University Press, New York and Oxford.

Vancini, F. (1997), "Thoughts on extended producer responsibility, innovation and eco-efficiency", Paper presented to OECD Workshop on "Fostering Eco-Efficiency: the Role of Government", Paris, 3-4 September (see Annex III).

Wallace, D. (1995), *Environmental Policy and Industrial Innovation: Strategies in Europe, the US and Japan*, Energy and Environment Programme, The Royal Institute of International Affairs. Earthscan, London.

Walley, N. and B. Whitehead (1994), "It's not easy being green", *Harvard Business Review*, May-June. pp. 46-52.

WBCSD [World Business Council for Sustainable Development] (1995), *Achieving Eco-Efficiency in Business*, Report of the World Business Council for Sustainable Development, Second Antwerp Eco-Efficiency Workshop, 14-15 March, WBCSD, Geneva.

WBCSD (1997), *Exploring Sustainable Development: WBCSD Global Scenarios* 2000-2050, Summary Brochure, WBCSD, Geneva.

von Weizsäcker, E.U., A.B. Lovins and L. Hunter Lovins (1997), *Factor Four*, Earthscan, London.

Wilk, R. (1997), "Emulation and global consumerism", in P. Stern, T. Dietz, V. Ruttan, R. Socolow and J. Sweeney, (eds.), *Environmentally Significant Consumption*, National Academy Press, Washington, DC, pp. 110-115.

World Bank (1997), *Expanding the Measure of Wealth: Indicators of Environmentally Sustainable Development*, Environmentally Sustainable Development Series and Monograph Studies, No. 17, The World Bank, Washington, DC.

WRI [World Resources Institute] (1997), *Resource Flows: The Material Basis of Industrial Economies*, Washington, DC.

OECD PUBLICATIONS, 2, rue André-Pascal, 75775 PARIS CEDEX 16
PRINTED IN FRANCE
(97 98 07 1 P) ISBN 92-64-16085-X – No. 50093 1998

QMW LIBRARY
(MILE END)